# *Ripoffs and Frauds*
How to Avoid and How to Get Away

Revised Edition

E. Thomas Garman

1996

DAME
PUBLICATIONS, INC.
Houston, TX

Cover Acknowledgement:
Appreciation is expressed to Roy Ramm,
Grade 6A, Frenchville State School,
North Rockhampton, Australia, who
developed the concept for the cover in a
1978 Consumer Education Poster Competition.

Legal Advice:
The information in this book is not intended to offer legal advice. The services of a competent attorney may be required to resolve a particular consumer problem.

Special Pricing:
Those who order bulk quantities of *Ripoffs and Frauds* may obtain a special price per unit. For information, contact Jan Tiefel, Dame Publications, 7800 Bissonnet, Suite 415, Houston, TX 77074; telephone 713-995-1000; fax 713-995-9637.

© **DAME PUBLICATIONS, INC.—1996**

First edition printed in 1995. Second edition printed in 1996.

All rights reserved. No part of this publication may be reproduced, stored in a retrieval system, or transmitted, in any form or by any means, electronic, mechanical, photocopying, recording, or otherwise, without the prior written permission of the publisher.

ISBN 0-87393-520-9

Printed in the United States of America

Table of Contents at a Glance

Preface		xiii
About the author		xv
Chapter 1	Why Ripoffs and Frauds Work Against Consumers	1
Chapter 2	How Ripoffs and Frauds Differ	9
Chapter 3	Telemarketing and Mail Scams	29
Chapter 4	Buying Ripoffs and Scams	37
Chapter 5	Vehicle Sales and Repairs	49
Chapter 6	Investment Swindles	53
Chapter 7	Legal and Moral Rights of Consumers	67
Chapter 8	How to Resolve Consumer Problems	75
Chapter 9	Laws on Sales Transactions	89
Chapter 10	Laws on Credit	103
Chapter 11	Laws on Vehicles	117
Chapter 12	Laws on Warranties	129
Chapter 13	Laws on Housing	133
Chapter 14	Sample Complaint Letters	139
Chapter 15	Agencies and Organizations That Help Consumers	147

Table of Contents

Preface xiii

About the Author xv

Chapter 1

Why Ripoffs and Frauds Work Against Consumers 1
    How Ripoffs and Frauds Work Against Consumers 2
    Why Ripoffs and Frauds Exist in the Marketplace 2
    What Do Deceptive Schemes and Scams Have in Common? 3
    General Guidelines to Avoid Ripoffs and Frauds 4
        Before Shopping 4
        When Shopping 5
        When in Doubt 6
    Consumer Update: Report Suspect Businesses to the Armed Forces Disciplinary Control
            Board 6

Chapter 2

How Ripoffs and Frauds Differ 9
    Ripoffs are Not Illegal 10
    Negative Option Buying Plans—Ripoffs? 11
    Rental Car Insurance—A Ripoff Industry? 11
        Rental Car Prices that Take You for a Ride 11
        Hidden Fees 12
        Overpriced and Unneeded Insurance 12
    Consumer Update: Cash-checking Companies that Offer Credit are Ripoffs 13
    Credit- and Debit-Card Registration Services—Ripoff? 14
    Credit Insurance (Life/Disability/Unemployment)—Ripoffs? 14
    Consumer Update: Photo Clubs for Military—Ripoffs? 15

Health, Diet, and Fitness Plans—Ripoffs?	15
Consumer Update: Vehicle Liability Insurance—Beware of Dealer Provided Choices!	16
Weight Loss Plans—Ripoffs?	16
Consumer Update: Job-Search Companies—Ripoffs?	17
Buying "As Is" Can Be A Ripoff	17
Telephone Company Ripoffs	18
Alternate Operator Services	18
Coin-Operated and Credit-Card Telephones	19
Inside Home Telephone Wire Maintenance	19
Making Long-Distance Calls	19
Consumer Update: 1-900-RIPOFF	20
Insurance (Health, Cancer and Life)—Ripoffs?	20
A List of Probable Ripoffs	21
Fraud Exists in the Marketplace	23
Consumer Update: Classified Advertisements are Full of Misrepresentations	24
Untrue, Deceptive, or Misleading Advertising Also Exists	24
Consumer Update: Advertising in Military Newspapers is Not Officially Sanctioned	25
Bait and Switch Advertising is Illegal	25
Puffery is Not Illegal	25
Misrepresentations Exist in the Marketplace, Too	26
Remedies Exist for Consumers Who Have Been Defrauded or Ripped Off by a Fraud or Misrepresentation	26

Chapter 3

Telemarketing and Mail Scams   29

Mail Frauds	30
Telemarketing to Get Your Money	30
Prizes and Free Gifts	31
Sweepstakes	32
Contests	33
Postcards Saying, "You Definitely Have Won!"	34
Many Charities Are Not What They Claim To Be	34
Consumer Update: The Gifts and Prizes ... What They Really Are	35

Chapter 4

Buying Ripoffs and Scams   37

Buying Clubs	38
Rent-to-Own	38
Consumer Update: Official Military Vendors Do *Not* Exist	39
Coupon Books	39
Vacation Certificates	40
Vacation Travel Clubs	41
Tour Operators	41
Scholarship Aid	42
Secured Credit Cards	42
Consumer Update: Encyclopedia Sales Contracts that "Cannot" be Canceled	43
Credit Repair Clinics that Promise to Erase Bad Information	43
Service Contracts—Not Worth the Money	44
Consumer Update: Free Rides for Military Personnel	45
Financing for Consumers with No or Bad Credit	46
Home-Related Scams	47
Second Mortgages Scam Against Homeowners	47

Chapter 5

Vehicle Sales and Repairs ... 49
Fictitious List Prices ... 50
Consumer Update: Subleasing Someone Else's Vehicle is Risky Business ... 50
High-Balling the Value of the Trade-in Allowance ... 50
Low-Balling the Price of the New Vehicle ... 51
Consumer Update: Odometer Fraud ... 51
Automobile Repairs ... 51

Chapter 6

Investment Swindles ... 53
The Investment Swindler's Game ... 54
Consumer Update: Watch Out for Telemarketing Recovery Room Scams! ... 55
Tips on Hows to Avoid Financial Swindles ... 55
Consumer Update: Financial Planning Seminars—Ripoffs? ... 56
Ponzi Schemes ... 57
Consume Update: Beware of "Educational Programs" on Insurance and Investments ... 57
Pyramid Schemes are Illegal ... 58
Consumer Update: The Airplane Pyramid Scheme ... 59
Multi-Level Marketing Investments are Legitimate ... 59
Chain Letters are Pyramid Schemes ... 60
Referral Rebate Sales are Pyramid Schemes ... 61
Precious Metals and Oil & Gas Deals ... 61
Penny Stock Schemes ... 61
Consumer Update: Information Highway Scams ... 62
Business Opportunity Schemes ... 63
Work-at-Home Scams ... 63
Deceptions and Biases in Financial Planning ... 64
Distant Land for Sale ... 64
Consumer Update: Financial-Advice Radio and Television Talk Shows ... 65
Timesharing Vacation Real Estate ... 65

Chapter 7

Legal and Moral Rights of Consumers ... 67
Legal Rights of Consumers ... 68
    Implied Warranty Rights are Powerful Legal Rights ... 68
    Warranty of Merchantability ... 68
    Warranty of Fitness for a Particular Purpose ... 69
    Express Warranty Rights are Enforceable ... 69
    Consumer Update: Unconscionability May Get One Out of a Contract Because the Seller Took Unfair Advantage of the Consumer ... 70
    Lots of Other Legal Rights Also Exist ... 70
    Consumer Update: Rule #1 of Consumer Life—When in Doubt About a Purchase, Put It on Your Credit Card ... 71
Moral Rights of Consumers are Legitimate Expectations ... 71
    General Moral Rights ... 71
    President Kennedy's Consumer Bill of Rights ... 72
    A List of Consumer Rights for All Americans ... 72

Chapter 8

How to Resolve Consumer Problems 75

    Why People Don't Complain 76
    Remedies to Resolve Consumer Problems 76
    How to Complain Effectively 77
    The Complaining Process Should Follow a Sequence 77
        1. The Local Business 79
        2. The Manufacturer 79
        Consumer Update: To Accurately Address Complaints, Use the *Consumer's*
            Resource Handbook 79
        3. Self-Regulatory Organizations 80
        4. Consumer Action Agencies 81
        5. Small Claims and Civil Courts 82
    Damages to Ask for When Suing 82
    Use a Class Action Lawsuit When Many are Wronged 83
    Alternative Actions for Consumers When Considering Breaking a Contract 84
    Consumer Update: Auto Sales Contracts—Read Before Signing 84
    Consumer Update: Yes! You Can Get Out of Many Contracts 85
    Use Small Claims Lawsuits to Sue When Necessary 85
    Consumer Update: Rental Car Company Violates Human Rights Law 86
    Techniques of Last Resort: How to Fight Back—And Win!—Against Deceptive Practices 87
    Consumer Update: How to Organize a Boycott 88

Chapter 9

Laws on Sales Transactions 89

    Laws and Regulations on Sales Transactions 90
    Telephone Solicitations Regulations of the Federal Communications Commission 90
    State Laws on Telephone Solicitation 90
    FTC Telemarketing Sales Regulations 91
    900-Number Federal Communications Commission Regulations 92
    Fight Back Against Ripoff Telephone Charges 93
    Unordered Merchandise Regulations of the Postal Service 93
    Negative Option Mail-Order Rule of the Federal Trade Commission 94
    Mail-Order Merchandise Regulations of the Federal Trade Commission 94
    Shopping by Telephone, Fax, and Computer 95
    COD (Cash on Delivery) Rule of the Postal Service 95
    Consumer Update: Free Magazine Subscriptions that Keep on Coming 96
    Door-to-Door Sales Regulations of the Federal Trade Commission 96
    Door-to-Door Sales Cooling-Off-Period State Laws 97
    Cooling-Off Laws for Health Spas, Timeshares, Campground Contracts, Mortgage
        Refinancing, Etc. 97
    Refunds Accompanying Cancellation of Contracts 98
    Consumer Leasing of Automobiles 98
    Airline Bumping Regulations 98
    Airline Lost Luggage Regulations 99
    Pet Lemon Laws 99
    Travel Club Laws 100
    Weight-Loss Center Laws 100
    Customer-Owned Coin-Operated Telephone State Laws 100
    Rent-to-Own Laws 101
    Deliveries and Installation Laws 101
    Testimonial Advertising Guidelines of the Federal Trade Commission 101
    Comparative Price Advertising Laws 102

Truth-in-Ticketing Package Tour Rule 102
Wheeler-Lea Act on Deceptive Advertising 102

Chapter 10

Laws on Credit **103**
    Laws and Regulations on Credit 104
    Limited Liability on Credit Cards 104
    Electronic Funds Transfer Act 104
        The Law Applies to Electronic Transfers, Debit Cards, and Credit Cards Used as
            Debit Cards 105
        Correcting Errors on Periodic Statements 105
        Lost EFT Cards 105
    Consumer Update: Your Present Homeowner's/Renter's Insurance Covers the Liability for
        Lost Credit and Debit Cards 106
    Automatic-Billing Disputes 106
    Fair Credit Reporting Act 106
        Rights Exist If Your Are Denied Credit 107
        All Consumers Have the Right to Know the Contents of Their Credit File 107
        Consumer Update: How to Get a Copy of Your Credit Report for Free 107
    Fair Credit Billing Act 107
        Consumers Get to Keep $50 of the Disputed Amount If the Credit Card Company Fails
            to Follow the Rules 109
        Reason #1 to Challenge a Credit Bill—Consumers are Not Liable for the Errors of Others ... 109
        Reason #2 to Challenge a Credit Bill—It Appears to be an Unauthorized Charge 110
        Reason #3 to Challenge a Credit Bill—Unsatisfactory Goods 110
        When Necessary, Consumers Should Write Firm Letters to Merchants and
            Credit Card Companies 110
    Consumer Update: Sample Complaint Letters to Resolve Credit Problems 111
    Equal Credit Opportunity Act 111
    Holder-in-Due-Course Doctrine 111
    Fair Debt Collection Practices Act 112
    Fair Credit and Charge Card Disclosure Act 112
    Consumer Update: You Can Refuse to Pay the Higher Rate When a Credit Card Company
        Raises Your Interest Rate 113
    State Laws on Credit Card Disclosures 113
    Home Equity Loan Consumer Protection Act 113
    Consumer Update: Why It is Difficult to Get Out of Secured Loans 114
    Consumer Update: Consumer Rights Under the Military Garnishment Law 115
    Home Ownership and Equity Protection Act 115

Chapter 11

Laws on Vehicles **117**
    Laws and Regulations on Vehicles 118
    Odometer Fraud Laws 118
    Motor Vehicle "Buyer's Orders" 118
    Lemon Laws for New Vehicles 118
    Consumer Update: Getting Out of Vehicle Contracts 119
    Used Vehicle Lemon Laws 120
    Used Vehicle Lemon Branding Laws 120
    Vehicle Repair Laws 120
    Secret Warranty Disclosure Laws for Automobiles 121
    Federal Trade Commission Used Car Rule 121
        Warranty Information in the Buyer's Guide 122
            A. "As is" 122

B. Implied Warranties Only	122
C. Warranties	123
Look for the Following Information on the Buyer's Guide	123
D. Full or Limited Warranty	123
E. Percentage of Repair Cost	123
F. Specific Systems Covered	123
G. Duration of Warranty	124
Unexpired Manufacturer's Warranties	124
Other Sections of the Buyers' Guide	124
H. Spoken Promises	124
I. Service Contracts	124
J. Prepurchase Independent Inspection	127
K. Vehicle Systems	127
L. Dealer Identification and Consumer Complaint Information	127
Additional Information	127
Private Sales	127
Spanish-Language Sales	128

Chapter 12

Laws on Warranties . . . 129

Magnuson-Moss Warranty Act	130
Standards for Companies that Offer Warranties	130
Disclaiming Implied Warranties is Prohibited	131
Full and Limited Warranties May Be Offered	131
Informal Dispute Procedures Are Encouraged	132

Chapter 13

Laws on Housing . . . 133

Laws and Regulations on Housing	134
Renter's Security Deposits	134
Late Possession of the Rental Property	134
Habitability of Rental Unit	134
Tenants Sometimes May Make Minor Repairs	135
Interstate Land Sales	135
Community Reinvestment Act	135
Fair Housing Act	135
Consumer Update: Community Reinvestment Act Ratings	136
Home Mortgage Disclosure Act	136
State Housing Discrimination Laws	136
Consumer Update: How to Identify Discrimination—Some Examples	137
Consumer Update: Help for Low-Income Home Buyers	137
Consumer Update: How to Report Discrimination	138

Chapter 14

Sample Complaint Letters . . . 139

How to Write a Letter of Complaint	140
Sample Complaint Letter to Merchant or Manufacturer	141
Complaint Letter to Dispute an Item on a Credit Card Bill	142
Complaint Letter to Merchant Requesting Credit for an Unsatisfactory Purchase	143
Complaint Letter to Credit Card Company About an Unsatisfactory Purchase	144
Second Complaint Letter to a Credit Card Issuer to Dispute an Item on a Credit Card Bill	145

Example of a "Consumer Statement" to Add to One's Credit Report to Tell the Consumer's
Side of a Dispute 146

Chapter 15

Agencies and Organizations That Help Consumers 147
Consumer's Resource Handbook 148
Federal Government Agencies That Help Consumers 148
State, County and City Government Offices That Help Consumers 155
Trade Association Resolution Programs 155

Preface

The marketplace is full of ripoffs and frauds that take advantage of consumers. Some are legal ripoffs—unfair, but not against the law. Others are fraudulent schemes and scams that are aimed at illegally separating consumers from their money.

Most schemes and scams are aimed at consumers in general, but it is well known that some sellers target certain groups of people with their ripoffs and frauds, such as military personnel, college students, recent immigrants, and the elderly. This book is designed to help all people, but especially military personnel and their families, better deal with ripoffs and frauds.

Most ripoffs and frauds can be avoided. To do so requires that you recognize them as ripoffs and frauds when you see them. This means that you need to be aware, informed and suspicious to the signs of ripoffs and frauds. Unfortunately, all such bad deals probably cannot be averted; therefore, eventually you are likely to get caught in a consumer ripoff or fraud.

The good news is that a great number of consumer problems can be fixed. To do so requires knowledge of consumer laws and regulations, an appreciation for the moral rights of consumers, and some effort to right the wrong. This will help you save money, too.

This book on *Ripoffs and Frauds* seeks to develop informed citizen-consumers who will stand up for their legal and moral rights as consumers in marketplace transactions. People must learn that they have many important consumer rights, some of which are very powerful. When used correctly, these rights can shift the balance of power away from the seller and in favor of the consumer.

This revised edition of *Ripoffs and Frauds* includes over a dozen addition deceptive schemes practiced by unscrupulous sellers. This revision also contains more than ten additional consumer protection laws and regulations, plus an example of a "Consumer Statement" letter to add to one's credit report to tell the consumer's side of a dispute.

Complaining and getting value for money—instead of getting ripped off—helps the individual consumer win! That's important because getting one's money's worth is the proper role of consumers in society. Complaining also helps improve the morality of the marketplace because most sellers will strive to improve their dealings with consumers as a result of complaints. Thus, consumers who make wise decisions in the marketplace, including complaining successfully, ultimately help raise the quality of life for all consumers.

Examples of ripoffs and frauds that specifically affect the military are featured in a number of boxed inserts in *Ripoffs and Frauds*. Special appreciation goes to Dean Brassington, Navy Family Services Center, Norfolk, Virginia, for being supportive of the idea to provide better consumer education for all military personnel. Dean is a course curriculum model manager and responsible for program development and standards for the U.S. Navy's Command Financial Specialist (CFS) training program. He supervises a talented team of financial educators whose activities include crisis counseling, training and education, and strengthening community partnerships. Dean was generous enough to provide for this book seven examples of how ripoffs and frauds impact the military. These are featured as boxed inserts.

Sincere appreciation is also expressed to additional experts for contributing information for other boxed inserts: Greg O'Donoghue, Manager, Personal Financial Management Program, Seymore Johnson Air Force Base, North Carolina; Jim Pressler, Hull Technician Chief, U.S. Navy; Paul Rubino, Financial Education Specialist, Norfolk

Navy Family Services Center, Norfolk, Virginia; Tom Snyder, Financial Counselor, Hurlburt Air Force Base, Florida; and, Carol Ann Walker, Personal Finance Manager/Air Force Aid Officer, Peterson Air Force Base, Colorado. Proofreading was done by the very able Michael D. Cox.

This book focuses on how to avoid ripoffs and frauds and, if caught in a ripoff or fraud, how to get away. Fighting back against consumer wrongs is very satisfying. It's also nice to win. Go for it!

E.T.G.

P.S. Readers are encouraged to share suggestions for change/improvement, plus offer additional examples of ripoffs and frauds. My mailing address is Virginia Tech, HIDM-0424-Blacksburg, VA 24061; the e-mail address is TGARMAN@VT.EDU for those who wish to communicate electronically.

About the Author

E. Thomas Garman is a professor of consumer affairs at Virginia Polytechnic Institute and State University in Blacksburg, Virginia. He received his bachelor's and master's degrees in business administration from the University of Denver and his doctorate in economic education from Texas Tech University. Garman's experience includes work for a United States Senator in Washington, retail sales management in Colorado, economic development project management in West Africa, and teaching for thirty-one years in eight states and four countries. Also, Garman has taught fifteen summer workshops for ten different universities, and seven of those were "Consumer Issues in Washington" classes taught on location in the nation's capital. He is a professor who truly enjoys teaching.

In 1994, Garman received the Stewart E. Lee Consumer Education Award from the American Council on Consumer Interests in recognition of his lifetime achievements in consumer education. In 1995, that same organization elected him a "Distinguished Fellow."

Garman has authored or co-authored 110 refereed articles and proceedings publications, 125 non-refereed publications, and thirteen books, including five currently available titles: ***Consumer Economic Issues in America, Fraud and Ripoffs: How to Avoid and How to Get Away, Regulation and Consumer Protection*** (the preceding with Dame Publications), ***The Consumer's World*** (McGraw Hill), and ***Personal Finance*** (Houghton Mifflin). His current writing project is ***Consumer Protection: Issues and Perspectives***.

Garman is a past president of two national organizations, the American Council on Consumer Interests and the Association for Financial Counseling and Planning Education, as well as one state professional association, the Consumer Education and Information Association of Virginia. He has made 77 major speeches to professional groups in 23 states and 3 foreign countries.

Garman has been a consultant to over forty corporations, trade associations and government agencies. He recently completed appointed terms of service for the National Advertising Review Board, the Consumer Advisory Council of the Board of Governors of the Federal Reserve System, and the National Advisory Council on Financial Planning for the International Board of Standards and Practices for Certified Financial Planners. Garman currently serves as a consultant for the U.S. Navy; as a member of the National Advisory Committee for "Money Over Fifty Program" of the American Association of Retired Persons; and, as a member of the Advisory Committee for the Consumer Credit Counseling Service of Western Virginia.

Garman teaches both graduate and undergraduate courses in consumer affairs and family financial management, fields in which his books are widely used. Garman has two grown children, and he lives with his wife in their home located on Gap Mountain near Newport, Virginia.

Chapter 1

Why Ripoffs and Frauds Work Against Consumers

What a wonderful economic marketplace we have in America. It provides us with thousands of good products and services. But sometimes the market is a tough place. As you no doubt have personally experienced, occasionally the marketplace seems intent on ripping off consumers, defrauding them, and separating people from their money. It happens, but it does *not* have to happen to you!

You can learn to spot the consumer problems in the marketplace and avoid them. It's important to see the ripoffs and frauds coming because if you don't see them, they are likely to catch you. And that will cost you money, too. Avoiding consumer problems is the better course of action.

If you get caught in a ripoff or scam, however, you can get out of most of these consumer problems. To get out of trouble, however, requires that you know how to do it. To correct a right after being wronged by a consumer problem, you must be armed with good information about your legal and moral rights as consumers. Such knowledge will empower you! Then stand and deliver your empowered consumer knockout punch so you can win.

This book will help you learn the games the bad guys use against consumers in the marketplace. Read on and avoid the problems. Learn how to protect yourself, your family and your friends.

How Ripoffs and Frauds Work Against Consumers

The purpose of business in the capitalistic economic system is quite clear: to make a profit. Theoretically, the goal of business should be to strive to do nothing else but satisfy the consumer, and the reward of profits should come its way. However, not every businessperson believes this. Businesses have to be vitally concerned with ongoing survival and prosperity, and most businesspeople know that the imperfections in the economic marketplace do not provide a "level playing field" among sellers or between sellers and consumers. For these and other reasons, some businesses practice ripoffs, misrepresentations and deceptions.

Economic theory suggests that competition is supposed to force dishonest businesses out of operation because consumers will refuse to buy from them and instead buy from honest ones. It stands to reason that if people find out who the honest ones are and buy only from them, the dishonest ones will be eliminated. After all, consumers who were once taken should not fall for the same deception again. But many of them do. And, dishonest business people have more than 263 million American shoppers as potential customers to choose from, including 2 million military personnel and 12 million students, and, therefore, do not need repeat customers—although the sad fact is that they often get them.

Today, one in six Americans reports being a fraud victim, according to a study by Princeton Survey Research Associates. The breakdown by age: 15 percent of people age 18 to 29, 20 percent of those 30 to 49, 18 percent of those 50 to 64, and 14 percent of those 65 years and older.

Why Ripoffs and Frauds Exist in the Marketplace

Ripoffs and frauds exist in the American marketplace for a number of reasons:

(1) Because of the irrepressible pursuit of self-interest and profiteering by some *unscrupulous sellers*; once the schemer has persuaded the potential victim that he or she needs something, the perpetrator will offer to satisfy that desire.

(2) A *lack of consumer knowledge* exists about common deceptions and misrepresentations, and this is why the potential victim is taken in by the encouragements to "act now." Otherwise, the consumer may investigate and discover the deceptive intent.

(3) The most common motivation on the part of consumers in deceptive situations is *greed*, since consumers often have a desire to get something for nothing or to get a lot for a little. There seems to be a universal desire to be healthy and wealthy.

(4) Some of the best frauds *make you feel stupid* if you do not accept the deal they are offering.

(5) Another factor is that many Americans today have what has been called a *sweepstakes mentality*. Part of the reason is that 34 states have lotteries and lots of people expect to win something for nothing. In a recent national survey, 11 percent of the respondents said that the best way to get rich was to play the lottery.

The U.S. Postal Service recently sent out pink-colored "sweepstakes postcards" to 200,000 consumers telling them that, "You are a winner! Congratulations!!" The card then listed "five wonderful prizes". Over 55,000 people called the toll-free number to claim their prize. "Winners" were played a tape recording advising them to be more

Chapter 1: Why Ripoffs and Frauds Work Against Consumers   **3**

careful about phony sweepstakes solicitations. This study means that about 30 percent of consumers reply to contest scams. A national survey by Louis Harris indicated that 29 percent of people contacted by the guaranteed prize postcard scheme have responded.

(6) We live in a complex economic marketplace where consumers make numerous decisions daily, and they *cannot possibly be well informed in all the areas of buying* that are necessary. Consumers who are ignorant about how to shop for best buys will not be able to follow logical and rational rules of consumption because they will get taken by the experts of unscrupulous selling.

(7) In addition, some deceptions, such as price fixing and other illegal forms of collusion to control supply, are *nearly impossible for the consumer to recognize*.

(8) Another difficulty is that most people think that magazines and newspapers will only accept *advertisements* from reputable sources. The reality is that if newspapers have no good reason to suspect an advertiser, they generally print the ad.

(9) The practice of deception is profitable for dishonest sellers because in today's economic marketplace they usually can make a lot of money before the authorities get around to investigating and prosecuting them. Probably *only two percent of victims ever complain* to the fraudulent sellers. Those sellers generally find it easy to satisfy the complaints of the two percent, and this usually can keep the government regulators at bay for some months or years. The unscrupulous sellers continue to profit by fleecing the next 98 percent who do not complain.

Making it more difficult, surveys show that fewer than 10 percent of consumers who say they were swindled report the crime to the proper government authorities. Many consumers—especially men—are too ashamed to complain.

(10) Many perpetrators of deception escape the effect of a state law by *fleeing from the boundaries of the state* and set up new businesses under different names to scam more victims. Penalties against deceptions are primarily civil in nature. When caught, perpetrators sometimes have their bank assets frozen, and such funds are used to make partial refunds to some consumers. But rare is the case when a criminal law is broken resulting in the bad guys serving jail time. Typically, perpetrators negotiate a settlement with a government, pay a civil fine, and move on, all the time avoiding criminal prosecution. The average life of scam business is as short as 30 to 90 days.

Since competition does not drive such sellers from the marketplace, society has to depend on the efforts of consumers to first, recognize and avoid such practices, and second, report any observed deceptive practices to the proper authorities. Moreover, for a variety of reasons, consumers fall prey to sellers who pretend to offer goods and services at competitive prices. Some deceptions are perpetrated by fly-by-night, out-of-town businesses, while others are practiced on consumers by well-known, so-called reputable businesses.

What Do Deceptive Schemes and Scams Have in Common?

Deceptive schemes and scams have similar characteristics. Misleading advertising is frequently used to lure consumers into deceptive schemes. People are led to believe that they are getting a really good deal, perhaps even getting something for free. Consumers are often fooled into putting up money for a good or service of inferior quality that is not a good value, and often is overpriced.

When consumers are enticed (sometimes after being told they are the "guaranteed winner" of a contest) to go to the sales office and listen to a sales pitch, they may be subjected to one or two hours of coercive sales tactics, including loads of false promises, and then be pressured into making a major purchase. Appeals to vanity are common. Also, shady sellers often tell lies when attempting to separate consumers from their dollars.

Consumers who are susceptible to deceptive schemes usually lack specific knowledge about the product or service, thus they are more vulnerable than others who are more informed. The consumer who is too trusting and does not ask critical questions becomes a victim. People must recognize that the purveyors of schemes and scams are experts at selling.

General Guidelines to Avoid Ripoffs and Frauds

Here are some guidelines to avoid ripoffs and frauds. In general, ripoffs and frauds can be avoided by using your common sense and a bit of healthy skepticism.

Before Shopping

1. Realize that nothing is *free*. It is almost impossible to get something for nothing. If the deal sounds too good to be true, it is. Beware of things that might be too good to be true. Check so-called bargains carefully.
2. Know your legal rights as a consumer, especially regarding implied warranties, door-to-door rescission, cooling-off periods, charge-back credit regulations, stop-payment check rights, and other remedies to correct wrongs.
3. Try not to be overly sympathetic to sales representatives, so as to avoid falling prey to deceptive practices using this tactic.
4. Avoid putting yourself in situations where you may be set up to be deceived, such as listening to sales pitches on the telephone or going to motels to hear sales pitches.
5. Be wary of purchasing from door-to-door salespersons.
6. Be alert to commonly-used deceptive practices, such as bait-and-switch advertising.
7. Be cautious about buying anything over the telephone. It is good advice never to buy over the telephone unless you originated the call or you know the caller.
8. Do not act on impulse by making quick decisions to buy or invest.
9. Read advertisements thoroughly, looking for limitations in the small print.
10. Educate yourself about the product or service you are considering buying and become aware of the likely prices involved. What does it do? What does it not do? Read such magazines as *Consumer Reports*, *Kiplinger's Personal Finance Magazine*, *Money*, *Smart Money*, and *Worth*.
11. Talk to friends and acquaintances to learn about their experiences with particular sellers, products and services.
12. While learning about a product you expect to buy, try to make up your mind as much as possible before you actually go shopping.
13. If desired, write to the Direct Selling Association (Mail Preference Section, P.O. Box 3361, Grand Central Station, 6 East 43rd Street, New York, NY 10017-4609) and ask to have your name removed from computer mailing lists; for telemarketing

solicitations write to the Telephone Preference Section at the same address. This takes approximately 3 months.
14. Consider the importance of and tradeoffs involved in buying good-quality products.

When Shopping

1. Buy from reputable sellers that you know. Get the name, address, and telephone number of either the salesperson or the company. In door-to-door solicitations, ask for proper identification and carefully examine it.
2. Check out the reputation of the seller by contacting the Better Business Bureau, the State Attorney General's Office, or an Office of Consumer Affairs. Telephone the same agencies in the state of any out-of-town sellers.
3. Always try to comparison shop for product features, price, and service at two or more sellers.
4. Ask lots of questions. Ask salespersons to explain advertisements, product operations, warranty terms, and so on.
5. Get verbal promises in writing.
6. Ask telephone solicitors to mail you information rather than discussing it over the telephone.
7. Never give your credit-card, checking account, or social security numbers over the telephone for "identification" or "verification" purposes, unless you initiate the call, have been a satisfied customer of the business in the past, or are certain of the caller's identity.
8. Never send cash, money orders or checks to a post office box or anywhere else unless you are sure about the company.
9. Never permit a courier service to come by your home or workplace to pick up cash, money orders or checks.
10. Pay no money in advance to obtain a loan.
11. Ask to see written warranties and read them. Understand the warranty before buying, such as what it covers, for how long, and who will honor it.
12. Ask to see the company's written policies on refunds and exchanges.
13. Ask what your legal rights are if you later want to cancel the contract.
14. Read and understand sales agreements and contracts before signing. Make sure the terms are the same as those given in the sales presentation, and get a copy of the documents.
15. If you do not like a particular clause in a contract, say so, cross it out, and get the initials of all parties next to the crossed out portion evidencing agreement that the clause is negated.
16. Realize that high-pressure sales tactics are a strong tip-off that you are the target of a scam.
17. Once you say "No" to a seller, stick to your position and leave the premises.
18. Do not allow yourself to be persuaded and pressured into hurrying and making a quick decision.
19. Ask the seller to give you time to think before you make up your mind, perhaps overnight.
20. Stop and think before buying. Consider, "Do I really need this?" "Why am I buying this?" "Does something sound a little fishy?" "Would I be smarter to ask a trusted friend before buying?"

21. Get a second opinion from a trusted friend or advisor on decisions of importance. Always try to get a second estimate for expensive repairs.
22. Get an attorney to look over important documents and contracts.

CONSUMER UPDATE:
Report Suspect Businesses to the
Armed Forces Disciplinary Control Board

The Armed Forces Disciplinary Control Board (AFDCB) has the power to act on complaints against businesses in its military district. On investigation of the complaint by a special agent, the business is advised that military members can be restricted from patronizing establishments that are seen to be fraudulent, discriminatory, or operating in any illegal or immoral manner. Essentially businesses are advised of the requirement of establishments to comply with the military Standards of Fairness if they wish to have military customers.

A business that continues to operate outside the best interests of military morale and welfare will be given a chance to defend itself in a hearing and change its business practices before being declared "Off Limits". A recent addition to the Hampton Roads Off Limits List for the military community was the buying club "Power Purchase". Buying clubs have great appeal to many young military consumers who either have not yet established credit or see the buying club service as an inexpensive method of one-stop shopping.

Mall kiosks often have attractive sales personnel (both women and men) who beckon to passing military members and encourage them to sign up. The salespeople receive commissions for each allotment they obtain. Military consumers are a great target for these sellers because of the allotment method of paying bills and the guaranteed payment by involuntary garnishments when voluntary payments are not made.

*Dean Brassington, Navy Family Services Center, Norfolk, Virginia

---

When in Doubt

1. When concerned about a possible deceptive situation, ask for advice from an impartial third person. Telephone the Better Business Bureau, State Attorney General's Office, District Attorney's Office, Bunco Squad of a Police Department, or an Office of Consumer Affairs to check the reputation of the seller and to verify claims made by a salesperson.
2. If you want to check the validity of a telemarketing call, ask the caller to mail you information and ask for a name and number to call back. Then check it out.
3. Never pay with cash. To cancel a check with a **stop payment order**, you need to telephone your bank before the check is presented for payment. If you pay with a credit card, you may have the legal right to not pay your credit-card company for poor-quality goods and services purchased from a seller.
4. If you must act "right now" to take advantage of a deal, don't. On important decisions, wait and talk to trusted friends.
5. When in doubt, don't!

Many people are embarrassed about being conned and deceived. Nobody wants to admit that he or she has been a fool, a patsy, or a mark. If you suspect you might have been taken, report it to the proper authorities. Chapter 8 discusses when and how to complain.

Not only will you probably not get your money's worth in some marketplace transactions, but also you may get into trouble because a number of schemes have contractual obligations. You can get out of some contracts, as noted in Chapters 8 and 11, but others may be impossible. When faced with a seller who apparently will not let you out of a contract, you might consider telephoning the state Office of Consumer Affairs or a local attorney for assistance. Most military bases and colleges have attorneys that, for no fee, assist people with consumer problems.

Chapter 2

How Ripoffs and Frauds Differ

There are dozens and dozens of ripoffs, misrepresentations, schemes, scams, flim flams, swindles, deceptions and frauds aimed at taking money from consumers. A few new ones are invented every year, too. These exist in all areas of the economic marketplace and this book will identify most of them.

Ripoffs, misrepresentations, and deceptions occur in all societies, especially where there is an almost inherent motivation among people to take advantage of others in economic transactions. The perpetrator's motivation for easy profits is only exceeded by consumers who seemingly want to take advantage of "a really good deal", or, better yet, "get something for nothing". The informed consumer must learn about the variety of schemes and ripoffs in an effort to avoid the come-ons, hooks, and traps used by unprincipled sellers.

Ripoffs, misrepresentations and frauds hurt the economy, sellers in the marketplace, and consumers. Instead of money being spent on valuable goods and services, resources consumed by deceptive schemes are wasted. Economic votes, in the form of dollars, are cast for unworthy products and services, and high-quality sellers are unfairly disadvantaged in an uncompetitive marketplace. It is in the interest of legitimate businesses and consumers to eliminate ripoffs and frauds.

Ripoffs are Not Illegal

Ripoffs are unfair acts of exploitation in the marketplace. Most often ripoffs involve paying prices that are too high or having little recourse when caught in an unfavorable situation. A company's product or service may not be purposefully designed as a ripoff, but the effect on a consumer may be exactly that—getting taken advantage of by not getting one's money's worth. Some examples:

- Paying $100 for a sweater that you see the next week in another store selling for only $70.
- Paying $6000 for a used car that's really worth only $4000.
- Signing a contract to "pay a few dollars a month" for a multi-year contract to receive several magazines of marginal interest that you later find out could have been bought at lower prices at a newsstand.
- Spending $30 a month on cable television and not watching 90 percent of the channels, but paying for them anyway.
- Paying $19.95 for a "special list" of government surplus property that is practically being given away (such as the infamous $44 Jeep), because it is also available free in a publication called, "Federal Sales Guide", that can be obtained from the General Services Administration.[1]
- Ordering $49.95 worth of vitamins advertised to "heal cold sores, prevent common colds, reduce hangover symptoms, and increase energy," only to discover that the claims were false.
- Saying "yes" to a caller asking you to buy light bulbs, trash bags or another household product to benefit disabled persons only to later discover that the price is five to twenty times its value.
- Paying a fee, perhaps $35, to electronically file your federal income tax return, with the result that the effective annual interest charged to obtain the refund in a few weeks is 80 percent or more.
- Paying $899 for a room full of furniture, only to find months later that the quality is so bad it is almost junk.
- Paying $29 for 8 ounces of "Dream Thigh Cream" that is supposed to melt away unsightly fat in days, only to realize that the product does not work.
- Expecting to find lower unit prices on larger quantity items, such as toilet paper, laundry detergent, and breakfast cereal, but discovering higher prices.
- Wasting 20 cents per gallon paying for high octane gasoline ($100 a year) when only 10 percent of today's cars require higher octane gas to perform correctly.
- Paying Ticketmaster Corporation $30 a ticket for a Pearl Jam concert even though the band wanted the price set no higher than $18.
- Being persuaded to pay for an extended service contract on a new television, VCR or automobile that pays off less than 2 percent of the time.

Ripoffs against consumers are a bad deal and they are unfair because buyers get little for their money. But, they are not illegal. Ripoffs may be exploitive, unethical, and

---

[1] A free copy may be obtained by writing the Consumer Information Center, Pueblo, CO 81009.

sometimes unconscionable, but they are generally legal. **Price gouging** is one form of ripoff, and it occurs when a seller charges an exorbitant price in a situation where the buyer has little, if any, option except to pay. For example, consumers staying at a hotel who find that the soda machine down the hall sells Pepsi for $1.25 a can. Having no choice at a sporting event except to pay $4 for movie popcorn and $3.50 for a drink are similar examples. In essence, the seller who price gouges takes advantage of his market power by exacting large markups. Until a judge says that a particular ripoff or price gouging circumstance is unconscionable, such practices are legal.

Negative Option Buying Plans—Ripoffs?

A **negative option plan** is a legal sales agreement between a consumer and a company that periodically delivers merchandise, such as books, compact discs, and videos. The contract obligates the consumer to accept and pay for an item unless he or she notifies the company within a specified time period that a particular item is unwanted. The advertisement may read, "Eight compact discs for $1.00!" When the offer is accepted, the consumer typically agrees to buy additional purchases under the club's negative option plan. If you want the selection offered, you do nothing; it will be shipped to you automatically. If you do not want the selection, you must tell the seller not to send it. The difficulty for consumers occurs when the negative option notice appears at their home address while they are away on vacation, or they simply neglect to return the notice, and it results in them having to pay for goods not wanted. This is known as "stop-us-before-we-mail-you-more-merchandise marketing." Ripoff![2]

A variation of the negative option technique is the **soft-sell** used by some of the nation's best-known companies who offer you either a free trial membership or complimentary copies of magazines. When the trial period is over, they assume that you want the membership or subscription service because you have not contacted them to say that you do not want it to continue. Then they bill you for an entire year. Companies selling long-distance telephone service sometimes use the same sales technique. This is trickery.

Rental Car Insurance—A Ripoff Industry?

Beware of the rental car industry because it is full of ripoffs, particularly in three areas: rental prices, hidden fees, and insurance.

Rental Car Prices that Take You for a Ride

Rental car prices are very confusing because the industry likes it that way. In many instances, you can get the best rental car price (even lower than the corporate rate) by ignoring the so-called discounts and telephoning around to make some cost comparisons.

---

[2]Once you fulfill the commitment to purchase so many items, you can request that you be switched to a positive-option plan. Then you get the catalog but do not have the obligation to return a postcard unless you want to purchase something.

Once you have a price quote and reservation in hand, simply show up at the rental car counter of a competitor and ask for a better price. This is known as the **walk-up price**. Try it and you will get a better price or a nicer vehicle, or both.

Hidden Fees

The typical rental car company assesses umpteen fees in the small print of the contract, such as charges for refueling, exceeding mileage limits, returning the vehicle late, city surcharges, airport surcharges, additional driver fees, under-age surcharges, child's car seat fees, bike rack charges, transporting fees to take customers from airports to rental offices, and late fees. These charges may add as much as 40 percent to the overall bill, yet they are never mentioned in the advertised rental rates.

Overpriced and Unneeded Insurance

In addition, rental car companies often use questionable selling techniques to peddle horribly overpriced insurance to consumers that often do not need the coverage. **Rental car insurance** are contracts sold through rental car companies designed to protect the consumer from bills if a rented vehicle is damaged or stolen. Rental car insurance has been called "a classic consumer ripoff" by the U.S. Public Interest Research Group (PIRG) because the coverage sold, sometimes using high-pressure sales techniques, is very expensive ($1.25 to $13.95 per day) and often duplicates the customer's private insurance coverage.

Rental car companies generally sell five types of overpriced insurance to consumers: (1) **Collision-damage waiver (CDW)** which pays if your rental car is damaged or stolen (and most drivers know it as collision insurance). This coverage has been banned in New York and Illinois, which wisely restrict the liability of drivers to $100 and $200. And, contrary to impressions received by many consumers, CDW does not cover bodily injury or personal property damage. (2) **Loss of use (LOU)**, sometimes called **loss-damage waiver**, which pays the rental car company for each day that the damaged rental car is in the repair shop instead of being rented to someone else. (3) **Personal accident insurance (PAI)** that pays for injuries to the driver or passengers. (4) **Personal effects insurance** or **personal effects coverage (PEC)** that protects against the theft of any personal items left in the vehicle. (5) **Additional liability insurance** which is an umbrella policy that provides up to $1 million for bodily injury and property damage caused to others in an accident.

Each of these insurance coverages run from $1 to $14 a day. Many uninformed consumers wind up paying these exorbitant charges that duplicate the coverage already provided by an employer's insurance (if the rental is for business use), available on their personal automobiles and homes, or provided automatically through credit cards and motor club memberships.

Smart consumers should take the following actions:

(1) Telephone your insurance agent and find out if your personal auto policy covers the potential types of losses that are possible when renting a vehicle. Obtain a copy of your insurance policy (with the appropriate section marked by the agent) to show if

needed; a copy is required for overseas rentals. Also confirm that your homeowner's (or renter's) insurance policy covers theft of items from rental cars.

(2) Telephone your credit-card companies to inquire about their automatic **secondary collision-damage** and **loss-of-use coverage** that provides insurance when a vehicle is rented using their credit card. Some credit-card companies, such as American Express, MasterCard and Visa, pay for the portion of damage to a wrecked rental car not covered by your personal auto insurance.

(3) If your present auto insurance policy does not provide adequate protection, ask your insurance agent to add a rider to your policy to cover collision and loss-of-use costs in rental cars. The cost? Only $20 to $30 a *year*—a whole lot cheaper than the rental car companies' daily fees! Also, be certain that you have liability insurance that covers rental cars, too.

The only people who should consider purchasing insurance coverage sold through rental car companies are consumers without auto insurance, those who are underinsured,[3] foreign visitors, and people who do not want to report a rental-car accident to their own insurance companies.

CONSUMER UPDATE:
Check-cashing Companies that Offer Credit are Ripoffs

Some check-cashing companies offer credit—at ripoff rates!—and such transactions are not illegal in all states. The typical deal offered by check-cashing businesses is to loan money to people who are short of cash by accepting a post-dated check from them. A **post-dated check** is a check written against a consumer's account and dated sometime in the future. The expectation is that the consumer will have sufficient funds in the account at that future point so the check will be honored by the bank. The check-cashing company (the "lender" here) charges exorbitant fees to advance funds against post-dated checks.

A typical transaction: On June 16th the customer presents a post-dated check for $260 and the company gives the consumer $200 in cash agreeing to hold the check until July 1st, two weeks later. On July 1st the consumer either pays the company $260 in cash or lets the check go through the banking system. The effective rate is 730 percent for two weeks, 1095 percent for ten days, and 2190 percent for five days.

One Attorney General observed that, "These companies are offering what are short-term loans with effective annual percentage rates of more than 2000 percent in some cases." They are targeting military personnel and civilians who are experiencing temporary financial difficulties.

Check-cashing companies are not legal lenders in most states. Consumers should avoid obtaining loans from such businesses, especially at exorbitant interest rates. The fees charged are a form of interest which should make the businesses subject to government regulation that would protect consumers.

*Greg O'Donoghue, Manager, Personal Financial Management Program, Seymour Johnson Air Force Base, North Carolina

---

[3] Be aware that some personal auto policies do not extend coverage to rental cars when the policyholder is on a business trip, although many business travelers are covered by an employer's policy.

Credit- and Debit-Card Registration Services—Ripoff?

In case of lost credit and debit cards, the cardholder should notify debit and credit card companies to avoid legal liability for fraud and misuse. Some firms sell a **card registration service** that registers all the credit- and debit-card numbers of a consumer and arranges for cancellation and replacement of any lost or stolen credit cards. For $25 to $60 a year, you only need to make one telephone call to report all card losses. While this may be a useful service to those consumers who do not keep a record of their credit cards, this is not an efficient purchase decision.

The Fair Credit Reporting Act (see Chapter 10) limits cardholder's liability to $50 in the event of a fraudulent use, and most creditors waive all costs in the event of fraudulent usage. In addition, every card issuer has a telephone number (most are toll-free) that you can call yourself to report a lost or stolen card and to get a replacement card. Further, almost all renter's and homeowner's insurance policies provide automatic coverage of up to $500 for lost or stolen credit and debit cards.

Credit Insurance (Life/Disability/Unemployment)—Ripoffs?

Most consumers are asked when they complete and sign a credit agreement whether or not they want to purchase credit life, disability, and unemployment insurance. Should the borrower die, become disabled or unemployed (according to the definition in the policy), the insurance pays off the unpaid balance of the consumer debt.

Finance companies and auto dealers sell this overpriced product to more than half their installment loan customers. The main reason is that sales commissions can exceed 70 percent of the premium. Some consumers do not even realize that they have purchased credit life, disability, or unemployment insurance. Others are mistakenly led to think that they cannot borrow without purchasing the insurance. Even if a lender requires coverage to secure a loan, the law says that the consumer need not purchase insurance from lender-recommended sources.

Credit life insurance is the nation's worst ripoff reports the Consumer Federation of America. An estimated $500 million is wasted annually on overcharges. State insurance commissioners have the power to regulate payout ratios, but most are lax. A **payout ratio** is the proportion of premium dollars paid out as benefits to insurance purchasers. A 65 percent payout ratio is the standard recommended by the National Association of Insurance Commissioners. Companies in some states pay out as little as 15 cents of every dollar in premium collected. What a ripoff!

The consumer's cost per $1000 of term life insurance purchased through a local insurance agent—those reputable people with an office on main street—likely would be 1/6 to 1/10 the amount of the so-called "small monthly premium" charged for most of these policies. The credit disability and unemployment coverage are equally costly. It is not uncommon for consumers to unnecessarily pay $2000 for life, disability and unemployment insurance premiums over the life of an installment loan.

Advice: Do not listen to the commission salesperson selling any of these insurance policies. Inexpensive term life insurance is available through credit unions and the military. Action recommendation: Before signing on the dotted line, use a pen to draw lines through anything that is not wanted; initial the changes. A few minutes of inattention can add up to many dollars of wasted money.

Chapter 2:   How Ripoffs and Frauds Differ   15

Military personnel may purchase the Service Man's Group Life Insurance (SGLI) for just about the lowest premiums possible. If you need a policy, contact local insurance sources, examine the coverage, read the policy, and compare prices.

> **CONSUMER UPDATE:**
> **Photo Clubs for Military—Ripoffs?**
>
> Photo clubs operate by mobile sales, mall picks-ups, and at-home sales. A typical sale begins with a car or van picking up walking sailors just outside of the base and transporting them to a mall or to the main sales office. There they will get a high pressure sales pitch. Many sailors are enticed by the attractive sales personnel. And the sales people are persuasive because they are experts at selling. The result is that the consumer signs an 18-month contract to purchase film, supposedly low-cost camera equipment, and photo albums. Later, the consumer often finds the same products and services available for much less money at the PX or NEX. However, once the contract has been signed, the consumer is legally committed to an allotment of perhaps $50 a month for 18 months, plus interest.
>
> Families fall for a similar sales pitch. Often a note is posted on doors or mailed announcing free prizes. The announcements look legitimate. A telephone call to the business may be followed by a sales visit by a young couple who insist on having the husband and wife present. The sales pitch is aimed at the emotions of providing family members with a record of their military lifestyle, complete with camera, film and albums for the time of the contract.
>
> The reality is that the same products are available, both on and off-base, at much lower prices. Plus, who do you know that spends $900 taking pictures except for a professional photographer? Think about it. Money not wasted on overpriced photo clubs can be diverted to the spending, saving and investing interests of the family instead of to the sellers. Many financial counseling clients involve allotment indebtedness to encyclopedia purchase programs, book/magazine subscriptions, and photo contracts.
>
> *Dean Brassington, Navy Family Services Center, Norfolk, Virginia

Health, Diet, and Fitness Plans—Ripoffs?

Health, diet, and fitness are an especially appealing areas for schemes since most people want to be in shape but few want to work to become trim and healthy. As a result, people are quite susceptible to health-related misrepresentations offering quasi-scientific claims like: "Lose 20 pounds a week with breakthrough diet!" "Regrow a full head of hair with foreign tonic!" "End arthritis pain with this stylish copper bracelet!" "Scrub away cellulite with ancient ingredient!" "Bleaching cream brightens your skin!" "Spray Slender Mist into your mouth to depress your appetite!" "Weight-loss secret from the Orient!" "Melt fat away while you sleep!" "Miracle cure for cancer!" "Bee pollen formula cures herpes!" "Home AIDS test!" Such advertisements ask for money and promise money-back guarantees.

Opting for such unproven pills, potions, drinks, gadgets, and programs may waste precious time that could be used for proven remedies and therapies. You can only be sure of four things in health quackery: (1) the product will not do what is promised, (2) your health may be harmed, (3) you will have wasted your money, and (4) you will not get a refund.

> **CONSUMER UPDATE:**
> **Vehicle Liability Insurance—Beware of Dealer Provided Choices!**
> The insurance choices offered by automobile dealers may not be best for consumers. Young and inexperienced military consumers are most likely to be ripped of by signing a purchase agreement which includes vehicle liability insurance. Such insurance often is written onto the preprinted contract to provide the appearance of legitimacy as a standardized procedure.
>
> While the car dealer can insist on vendor's liability insurance to protect their legal interest in the property until it is fully paid for, the buyer does not have to buy insurance from the seller. This fact is glossed over by some dealers who offer insurance as a "convenience" for the customer.
>
> Potentially dangerous is the misleading assumption that the liability portion of the insurance provided by the dealer provides an adequate amount of property damage and bodily injury liability coverage. The typical dealer provided liability insurance offers only the minimum amount of liability coverage required by state law—perhaps as low as $10,000. Unfortunately, many a sailor has been tragically awakened to the fact that in the absence of proper liability coverage, they are liable for $25,000, $50,000, or more after an accident. If you need a policy, contact a local insurance source, examine the coverage, read the policy, and compare prices.
>
> *Dean Brassington, Navy Family Services Center, Norfolk, Virginia

Weight Loss Plans—Ripoffs?

An estimated 50 million Americans will go on a diet this year. While some will succeed in taking off weight, very few—an estimated five percent—will manage to keep all of it off in the long run. The only way to lose weight and keep it off is to eat fewer calories or use more calories. This can be done by eating less food, exercising more, or both. There is no magic bullet to eliminate fat from the system.

Quackery succeeds in this $30 billion industry because there are so many customers who are willing to try some new diet book, pill, cream, or something they think might work. Ideas that do not keep the weight off include diets that focus on one particular food, such as grapefruit; pills, such as starch blockers, advertised as diet aids; electrical muscle stimulators; body wraps, preceded by application of some cream or lotion; and pills and capsules that promise to burn, block, flush or otherwise obliterate fat. Rapid weight-loss programs can jeopardize a dieter's health, as well as one's wallet. Last year General Nutrition Centers, Inc., the largest retailer of nutritional supplements in the U.S. was fined $2.4 million to settle federal allegations about deceptive claims on over 40 products sold in its 1,500 stores. Also last year the Federal Trade Commission accused some of the makers of very low liquid-diet programs (New Directions, UWCC Permance Program, HMR Fasting Program) of falsely claiming that their products were risk free; the ads were stopped.

Commercial diet programs, such as Jenny Craig, Nutri-System, and Weight Watchers are not very successful at helping people keep weight off either. A National Institute of Health panel reviewing industry-supplied data found that dropout rates go as high as 80 percent. While many commercial programs help people lose ten percent of their body weight, they all fail over the long term. That's why the Federal Trade Commission recently filed complaints against most of the well-known diet program companies for false advertising.

This is a multi-billion dollar industry that offers consumers products that do not do what people expect. Typically, government can step in alleging violations of the law when products are specifically harmful to people's health or the advertising is clearly deceptive.

CONSUMER UPDATE:
Job-Search Companies—Ripoffs?

Unscrupulous sellers also take advantage of people who are seeking employment, such as some job-search companies. Because people may be experiencing difficulty in locating a job, they sometimes turn to private employment agencies. The process works like this: The person completes an application form and signs a contract to register interest in certain types of jobs. The **job-search company** then provides some career counseling, helps improve the person's resume, and tries to locate suitable job positions for which the person can interview. Most headhunters, executive recruiters, management consultants, and outplacement firms are reputable businesses; some are not.

The way some of these companies make money is to charge a fee, often $500, $1000, $2000, or more, for trying to place someone in an employment position. Ads tucked away in classified sections entice consumers by claiming they can open hidden jobs or boasting about secret connections, sometimes with overseas employers. Most of the disreputable firms offer nothing more than sloppily done resumes and outdated lists of corporate contacts. Some firms go through the motions of forwarding your resume in an attempt to help you find a job; others require that you send out your resumes. The small print in the signed contract spells out the limitations, such as printing costs are an extra charge and that the firms do not guarantee clients jobs. The job seeker must pay any remaining fees "when the person accepts a job of his or her choice," no matter how it was found.

The unethical career counselors make big promises about getting job interviews, sometimes even charging a surcharge of 10 percent to guarantee a new job within 6 months; then they do not deliver. Most legitimate employment agencies collect no fees in advance from those looking for work. They only get paid if and when the person finds employment for which the agency arranged an interview. Reputable agencies typically collect their entire fee from the employer, not the new employee. Some states prohibit fees from being paid ahead of time before a job is taken; others prohibit employment firms from collecting fees from employees.

Buying "As Is" Can Be A Ripoff

"**As is**" means that the buyer assumes full responsibility for determining the condition of a product being purchased and releases the seller of all legal claims. There is nothing wrong or illegal with selling some products "as is", because the consumer usually has a choice to buy a similar product with an implied warranty or other guarantee. For example, one might buy a used vehicle for a very low price on an "as is" basis. Alternatively, for a much higher price one could buy a similar car that has a warranty. If the "as is" car was purchased and it turns out that the vehicle actually was in excellent condition, the buyer got a great buy; if the buyer purchased the "as is" car and it quickly turned out to be a terrible car, the buyer got ripped off.

A deception could arise should a consumer buy something "as is" without knowing that the "as is" phrase appears in the small print of the contract. Many states have regulations governing "as is" merchandise, requiring that such items be conspicuously marked "as is". Consumers often sell each other vehicles on an "as is" basis.

Telephone Company Ripoffs

The telephone business is competitive, but unfortunately for consumers in some corners of the market companies are competing not to offer the lowest rates. Instead, they are offering telephone services for the highest prices they can charge.

Alternate Operator Services

Alternate operator services (AOS) are a relatively new segment of the telecommunications industry and they are pushing up the prices of long-distance telephone services for consumers who make credit-card and third-party billing calls. After buying some switching equipment and hiring some operators, these companies lease long-distance lines from the major carriers and enter into contracts with businesses such as hotels, motels, airports, hospitals, and universities to resell standard intrastate and interstate long-distance telephone services. In many cases, the AOS company charges exorbitant prices, often from two to ten times the traditional cost of making a long-distance telephone call, such as through AT&T, MCI, or U.S. Sprint.[4] This occurs even if you call collect or charge the call to your telephone credit card. The approximately 90 AOS companies share their profits with the owners of the businesses with whom they contract. Today, one in six publicly available phones is an AOS telephone.

If you are ripped off by these charges, you can complain to your local telephone company and refuse to pay the exorbitant amounts charged. The local companies, which are required to do the billing for the AOS companies, are allowed to offer credits to complaining customers.

A Federal Communications Commission (FCC) order requires AOS companies in interstate commerce to inform users of the services how much calls will cost. They must put identification on or near the telephone. The FCC also ordered them to not block callers from using other long-distance carriers, if the customer requests. So far, the FCC has chosen not to regulate rates. Consequently, if you are in a motel and are going to make a lot of telephone calls, you might consider making your calls from a public telephone. When in doubt, dial 0 to reach a local telephone company operator or 00 to reach a long-distance operator and ask about the cost of the call.

---

[4]Consumers in most states who need assistance in dealing with their telephone shopping requirements may call the Tele-Consumer Hotline (800-332-1124) for help. Supported by industry and consumer groups, the organization answers questions about phone services and mails consumers fact sheets. For $2, Telecommunications Research and Action Center (202-408-1400) will send you a cost comparison of the major plans; TRAC, P.O. Box 12038, Washington, D.C. 20005.

Coin-Operated and Credit-Card Telephones

Calls placed from the nation's nearly 2 million pay telephones are now deregulated. Owners of premises that have pay telephones receive a commission (usually 15 percent) on the local and long-distance charges that callers ring up. Companies are selling their new telephones and contracts to hotels, motels, airports, truck stops, drugstores, gas stations, universities, hospitals, and prisons. The premise owner's incentive is to choose the telephone equipment that charges the highest rates. The marketplace does not promote competition when the owner of the telephone is not its primary user—ripoff.

Inside Home Telephone Wire Maintenance

Another telephone company ripoff is the price charged for inside wire maintenance and repairs. Local telephone companies charge between $1 and $2 a month, often lumped into the monthly service amount on your bill. If there is a service problem with the telephone wire inside your home, the telephone company will repair it.

On average, you will need this service once every 15 to 20 years. For every dollar collected by the telephone companies, they keep about 85 cents for profit, thus, the price is astronomical compared to the economic value of the service. About 2/3 of telephone customers have maintenance plans, and about 1/3 of them do not even know that they are paying for the plans.

The state government regulatory agencies presume that this service is competitive and that competition will regulate prices of services offered. In some states, customers must affirmatively act in order not to be billed for inside wire maintenance services. This is called an "**op out plan**".

Making Long-Distance Telephone Calls

Those who frequently make long-distance calls (more than $10 a month) should consider signing up for one of the various "discount" programs advertised by the long-distance telephone companies. Only 30 percent of households have signed on, perhaps because of the confusion associated with the rates and the advertising. The companies often offer cash and free long-distance minutes to switch from one carrier to another. Every year about 16 percent of U.S. households switch telephone companies.[5]

Another alternative is to buy service from a **long-distance reseller**. These are firms that buy long-distance time in bulk from the major carriers and sell those minutes to consumers. You may not recognize these companies as household names, but their prices are low.

The person who makes only a few long-distance telephone calls per month pays the highest rates when compared to others. Historically, low-volume telephone users have had little choice since only heavy users of telephones are given preferential rates. Now they can use **telephone dumb cards** which are low-tech telephone cards that permit the use of a preset number of prepaid telephone minutes at a flat rate per minute. Calls made on a prepaid card are usually lower than dialing zero and using a credit card, but only

---

[5]The illegal practice of **slamming**, the unauthorized switching of a customer's long-distance telephone service, continues in the industry with more than 3000 annual complaints to the Federal Communications Commission.

if you keep calls short (under four minutes) and make them during the day, when standard rates are the highest. Avoid getting ripped off by being aware that prices vary widely, generally from 60 cents per minute all the way down to 10 cents.

> **CONSUMER UPDATE:**
> **1-900-RIP-OFF**
>
> The over-the-phone information services industry is growing rapidly. Numerous firms promote services that are desired by somebody out there and accessible by telephone. Most services are outrageously overpriced. People pay money to listen to recordings and/or talk with others about astrology, murder confessions, sex, engine overhauls, Easter bunnies, and chat with well-known people, like baseball player Jose Canseco or the Vatican's Pope. You can even play a round of "Let's Make a Deal". Although not illegal, when the bills get high, family members are dismayed when they discover that someone in their household spent $100 or $400 last month dialing 900- and 976-numbers. One observer wrote of these numbers, "1-900-RIP-OFF."

Insurance (Health, Cancer, and Life)—Ripoffs?

Advertisements in the Sunday newspapers, in various magazines, and on television make fantastic claims about the need for insurance protection against the likelihood of death, cancer, and other dread diseases. Usually a celebrity, movie star, or athlete makes the promotion. And they may get $100,000 or more for one day of taping commercials.

All too often these people are pitching nearly worthless health and life insurance policies. Suggestions that, "One out of three people will get cancer" and that "The average hospital stay for cancer victims is 2 months" are pure fabrications. Companies tell such lies to create illusions and fears that they promise to fix. They may claim that, "Cash benefits are paid directly to you" or "No one can be turned down for life insurance." Then they set artificial time limits, such as, "You must apply by October 15!" or buried in the small print, "No benefits for two years." Mail-order insurance is largely a world of schlock.

The products being advertised are called **supplemental health insurance** and **term life insurance**. The ads mention the initial benefits, such as guaranteeing acceptance and providing $10,000 to $50,000 in life insurance coverage, and then fail to tell crucial details—what several insurance commissioners have called serious misrepresentations and omissions. The state of Washington has tough advertising standards and has prohibited the broadcast of commercials from many of these companies, arguing that they were "false, deceptive, or misleading advertisements."

Typically the insurance is poorly explained and quite expensive compared with policies sold by local insurance agents. These advertised policies often contain severe restrictions and limitations on the coverage provided.

About the life insurance policies, Robert Hunter, insurance expert for the Consumer Federation of America, says that most of these policies pay nothing if the policyholder dies within the first two years and then only $1500 on the non-accidental death of a

A LIST OF PROBABLE RIPOFFS

Ripoff	The Promise Explained	The Reality
Fake Checks	The check made out to you; also stamped "This is not a check"	Can only be used to purchase over-priced products from a catalog
False Gold and Platinum Credit Cards	$49.95 membership fee for a "similar" card	Can only be used to purchase over-priced products from a catalog
Low-Interest Credit Card	$99 permits you to transfer other credit balances to the low-interest card	If a real Visa or Mastercard is received, the rate will rise later; most often the consumer receives a booklet explaining how to apply for a card
Unordered Merchandise	Company mails something with the hope that receiving party will pay	You may keep anything shipped to you and then you can assess the sender storage fees and charges to return the goods
Phony Bills	Bill comes in the mail, perhaps for a deceased relative	A likely fraud; ask for copy of a signature on order form
Unclaimed Funds	Letter on official-looking stationery saying a "routine audit" has determined that you are owed money; send $35 for processing fees	Only scam artists charge processing fees
Going Out-of-Business Sales	Sign looks legitimate and the store seems full of goods	Lots of poor quality merchandise brought in when liquidating a legitimate business; must be licensed
Home Improvements and Repairs	Promises high-quality work and must have X dollars as a down payment	Unlicensed repairpersons take the money and run; sometimes they just do shoddy work with poor materials
Free Baby Photos	Company offers free baby photos but pressures the consumer to buy expensive photo packages	Take the free photos and pay an inexpensive service charge; skip the package deal
Magazines	Young people sell magazines pretending that they are working their way through school	Either one overpays for the subscription or the "salesperson" disappears with the money

Vacuum Cleaners, Sewing Machines, Encyclopedias, and Fire Extinguishing Systems	Usually legitimate door-to-door sales of consumer goods	Often horribly overpriced and the merchandise is not needed
Campground Memberships	Consumer signs 25-year lease to use same plot in campground for two weeks every year	Overpriced and not really needed; companies often go bankrupt
Health Club Spas, Weight-Loss Center, Martial Arts Facilities, and Dance Lessons	Consumer signs a contract for a series of services and some success is quickly achieved	Firm often cannot deliver what was promised; many companies go bankrupt
Freezer Meat	Very low advertised price for frozen meat	Meat sold at "hanging weight" before fat is cut off; poor quality meat is substituted when packed
Frozen-Food Freezer Plan	Bulk purchase of meat delivered regularly and it includes purchase of freezer	Freezer is overpriced; quality of food is excellent in the beginning, then declines
Degree Mills	Sell diplomas for a price with an extreme minimum of on-site educational experiences	Such diplomas do not meet the standards of the genuine accrediting associations
Term Papers	Sell term papers on any topic	Poorly written and referenced essays that if turned in to a school will result in disciplinary action
Song Writing and Vanity Publishing	Promise to publish your work and you can expect to make royalties on the sales	Firm collects substantial upfront fee that pays the cost of production; profits never exist
Phony Bank Examiner	Asks for help in identifying teller who is embezzling funds by having consumer make withdrawal from that teller	The receipt from the "bank examiner" is worthless because he really does not work for the bank
Pigeon Drop	Person "finds" money in a bag or envelope and offers to share it with a nearby consumer	After taking "pigeon's" good-faith money to a lawyer's office for safekeeping, the bag of money is switched; a partner is often used and the lawyer does not exist
Work at Home	Advertisements for huge profits for at-home tasks	Products completed at home often refused by seller; sometimes the "deal" requires consumer to run similar ads to get money from other consumers

60-year-old man. To keep the premiums level, the benefits also drop with age. For example, the policy advertised by one television actor pays only $500 at age 65 and only $350 at age 70. A study by the state of Wisconsin found that only three policyholders in 1000 collect in the first seven years.

These ads continue partly because most state insurance commissioners and legislators are reluctant to write regulations that are strict enough to get them off the air. Compared to standard policies in the industry, such mass-marketed policies are a ripoff—you pay way too much for what you receive. People who have life insurance coverage through their employment or who already have a private policy do not need mail-order policies.

Most advertised health policies duplicate coverage that consumers already have, restrict the conditions for paying a claim, do not pay for preexisting conditions for the first two years the policy is in effect, pay minuscule benefits, and pay nothing until the insured has been in the hospital 14 days. These types of health insurance policies simply do not provide the insurance protection that consumers think they are getting. Such policies are just ripoffs. Further, the purchase of inadequate insurance coverage lulls many consumers into falsely thinking that they are properly insured when, in fact, they are not.

Consumers who already have major medical coverage as part of their health insurance plan are already adequately covered for illness, including cancer. Major medical coverage can be added to most health insurance policies, if it is not there already, for perhaps another $30 per month.

The National Association of Insurance Commissions (NAIC) reports an industry-wide payout ratio of 37 percent for mail-order health insurance policies. A **payout ratio** is the proportion of premium dollars paid out as benefits to insurance purchasers. That means, industry-wide for these types of policies, for every dollar paid in premiums policyholders only receive 37 cents through claims. This horrible return does not come close to the NAIC payout ratio standard of 65 percent for policies sold directly to consumers and 75 percent for policies sold to groups. Policies with low pay-out ratios are ripoffs. If you need a policy, see a local source for insurance, examine the coverage, get confirmation on the payout ratio (from the state insurance commission, if necessary), read the policy, and compare prices.

Fraud Exists in the Marketplace

A **deception** is a form of trickery involving the selling of goods or services to consumers. Efforts to stop consumer deceptions depend greatly on the definition used by the Federal Trade Commission. This is because the Uniform Commercial Code, as well as the deceptive practices acts in many states, accept the federal definition. Historically, the FTC defined **deception** broadly as, "a tendency or capacity to deceive." Using this standard to protect all consumers, the FTC did not have to prove actual deception or definite injury to consumers. Since 1983, the FTC more narrowly defined **deception** as a material "representation, omission, or practice that is likely to mislead the consumer acting reasonably in the circumstances, to the consumer's detriment." **Material information** is information that is important to reasonable consumers and which is likely to affect their choice of a product or service, such as express statements about the product's cost, safety, quality, effectiveness, performance, durability, and warranty protection. This newer definition of deception places an increased burden of proof on consumers and government consumer protection agencies.

Legally, **fraud** (or **deceit**) is a deliberate deception practiced in order to secure an unfair or unlawful gain or advantage where the seller intentionally misleads the buyer. Here the buyer must have relied on the word of the seller as being true. Fraud comes about when a

> **CONSUMER UPDATE:**
> **Classified Advertisements are Full of Misrepresentations**
> Classified advertisements placed in newspapers and at the back of magazines are almost never investigated for truthfulness by the owner of the publication. As a result, this form of advertising attracts unscrupulous sellers.
> Popular scams regularly seen in classified ads include:
>
> - Overseas employment opportunities (you pay an **up-front fee** [also called an **advance fee**] for names of potential employers)
> - Loans for consumers with poor or no credit history (advance fees are charged, and if you get a loan it will be at an extremely high interest rate)
> - Earn money by working at home (promoter sells overpriced goods for you to work on and then does not buy them back when completed)
> - Phony education scholarships (you pay for a worthless outdated book listing scholarships for which you will not qualify)
>
> You can be confident of two things when responding to a classified advertisement: (1) the reality will not be the same as what was advertised, and (2) you will not get your money back, even though the promoter "guaranteed" that refunds would be available.

knowing deception causes the consumer to enter into a transaction, and by doing so the consumer suffers a financial loss.

Several elements must be proven to show fraud, and this is why it is so difficult to prove a case of consumer fraud in a court of law:

- false representation,
- knowledge that the facts stated were untrue,
- intention to deceive the victim,
- actual belief on the part of the victim, who is ignorant of the falsity of the representation, that the false representations are true, and
- damages suffered by reliance on the untruths.

All states have consumer protection acts that protect consumers against deliberate frauds. Fortunately, most states are more generous in their definition of fraud than the federal government, in that they provide that practices are fraudulent if they have a "capacity or tendency to deceive," even if they do not actually deceive. Thus, practices may be deceptive "if the ignorant, the unthinking, and the credulous" could be deceived. States with a broader definition, therefore, have the power to prohibit marketplace behaviors that are "unfair" as well as deceptive. Moreover, the broader definition helps protect specific types of consumers who might not be shielded under the more narrow standard-children, the elderly, and those whose first language is not English. States with the broader definition do a better job of protecting consumers.

Untrue, Deceptive, or Misleading Advertising Also Exists

Deceptive practices are considered fraudulent, and are against the law, when the statement, omission, or practice is likely to mislead a consumer. In the area of advertising, for example, the Federal Trade Commission (FTC) can find that silent omissions are materially deceptive when sellers tell only half truths. The FTC's current standard for deception rests on what a *reasonable consumer* would do. The FTC decides advertising deception on a case-by-case basis. In states where the statute more broadly protects consumers from deception, the state attorney general can fight deceptive advertising that escapes the FTC's definition.

CONSUMER UPDATE:
Advertising in Military Newspapers is *Not* Officially Sanctioned

Since a business has advertising in a military newspaper, it must be OK, right? Nope! Details can be found in the rarely read disclaimer, typically located on the second page of the newspaper, which states that the content does not represent the views or imply endorsement by the Department of Defense. Those free military newspapers are a contracted service and the papers are under no obligation to check out the honesty of every company that advertises. Ads for vehicles make up much of the revenue for military newspapers. Consumers must realize that both good and bad businesses place advertisements in newspapers.

*Dean Brassington, Navy Family Services Center, Norfolk, Virginia

---

Bait and Switch Advertising is Illegal

Bait and switch advertising is the offer of goods or services at bargain prices when the seller has no intention of selling the advertised products, but instead desires to sell a substitute at a higher price. Sometimes the seller pushes an inferior substitute at an exorbitant price. The bait is the product or service advertised at the apparently low sale price in order to lure the customer into the store. The well-meaning consumer wants to take advantage of the bargain, but the salesperson almost always refuses to sell the product, for such reasons as..."There aren't any left," "You can't get delivery for 3 months," "Many people who bought it aren't satisfied," and "The product just isn't very good." Instead, the salesperson persuades the customer to buy a similar but more expensive item. This is the switch.

Do not confuse bait and switch with **trading up**, since this is a perfectly proper sales technique where a salesperson encourages a customer to buy a higher-priced item in order for the salesperson to make a bigger sale, earn a larger commission, and/or better fill the customers needs and wants. Sometimes there is a fine line between trading up and bait and switch selling practices.

Puffery is Not Illegal

One must not jump to the conclusion that a fraud has occurred whenever a false statement is made, however. Loose statements and exaggerations concerning the quality, value, or goodness of a product may be considered sales talk or puffery. **Puffing** involves exaggerated statements and opinions by a seller as to the quality or value of an item offered for sale that is not made as a representation of fact. Puffing is not considered fraud in the eyes of the law, since everyone knows a seller will tend to exaggerate a bit. Sellers are allowed some leeway in describing attributes of their products, and such overstatements are typically considered innocent misrepresentations. Statements such as, "This is the finest-quality wool coat money can buy," "This is the most powerful vacuum cleaner made in America," and "There is not a bit of rust on this five-year-old car" should not be taken seriously by consumers.

Misrepresentations Exist in the Marketplace, Too

A **misrepresentation** is the reporting of something by words or conduct in a mistaken or false manner that is not in accordance with the facts. This includes relevant omissions as well. Most misrepresentations, even outright lies, are not considered fraudulent by the courts. The ways in which products and services are being offered to the consuming public are often misleading because the whole truth is generally not told. Most people would agree that misrepresentations are pervasive in the American marketplace.

Someone making a misrepresentation with an intentional false statement of fact-generally made as an inducement to contract-is committing fraud. Proving fraud, however, requires the speaker's knowledge of the falsity of the statement and an intent to deceive, and such concrete examples of such deception probably do not occur very often.

More often what happens in marketplace transactions is that a seller innocently, but mistakenly, represents something to be true that is not. When such negligent, innocent, mistaken and unintentional false statements are made as an inducement to contract, it generally is considered in common law to be an instance of **constructive fraud**. Why? Because such inducements are highly unfair to consumers. Still, the burden is upon the consumer to prove fraud.

Remedies Exist for Consumers Who Have Been Defrauded or Ripped Off by a Fraud or Misrepresentation

To combat some of the difficulties in proving fraud and to make it easier for governments to protect consumers, all states have a general consumer protection statute that applies to "consumer transactions" which addresses both intentional and unintentional misrepresentations. Such statutes include provisions against negligent misrepresentations because it would be unfair to consumers if someone making false statements, even innocently, reaped the benefits of such representations. In addition, states have a variety of specific statutes that attack particular consumer problem areas, such as health spas, campground memberships, employment services, and auto repairs. (Illustrative laws are noted in Chapters 9 through 13.)

These state laws empower the Attorney General, government attorneys (county, city or town) and/or the head of the Office of Consumer Affairs to investigate and prosecute potential violations of the consumer protection statutes in that state. They may sue for injunction, civil penalties, costs, and restitution for wronged consumers. Most consumer protection statutes provide for civil penalties, rather than criminal sanctions. Importantly, many of the statutes also empower the wronged consumer to take legal action against the perpetrators. Under some statutes, the winning consumer may win damages and get his or her attorney's fees paid by the defendant.

Thus, remedies exist for people who are induced by deception or misrepresentation to spend their money unwisely and/or enter into contracts. Consumers may obtain relief in instances where honest misstatements by sellers cause misunderstanding as to the characteristics or benefits of items offered for sale. To prevail, the buyer must show that the statement was relied on and that he or she suffered damage.

Consumers usually have two choices of remedy. First, wronged consumers might sue for **restitution**, an amount of money to restore something that has been taken away, lost, or surrendered. Note that the state government (Attorney General or Office of Consumer Affairs) may do this for you and other wronged consumers. Second, a consumer may try to **rescind** the contract, which is getting out of it by repealing or annulling the contract and making it void.

Depending upon the circumstances, consumers may also ask for damages, such as for out-of-pocket losses, pain and suffering, and expenses incurred as a consequence of the problem. Every year, court decisions at the federal, state, and local levels, and government regulatory actions, help consumers by stopping thousands of deceptive practices, getting people out of bad contracts, and, in a few cases, obtaining refunds. Recognize though that most money spent on deceptive selling practices is lost.

Chapter 3

Telemarketing and Mail Scams

Several types of ripoffs, misrepresentations, and deceptions regularly use the mails and telecommunications as ways to reach consumers. Examples include mail frauds, telemarketing promotions, prizes and free gifts, sweepstakes, contests, postcards saying, "You Definitely Have Won!", and charities that are not what they claim to be.

Mail Frauds

The Postal Service reports that the average American gets 250 pieces of junk mail, mostly advertising materials, every year. That amounts to over 40 pounds of catalogs, political flyers, charitable solicitations, sweepstakes packets, magazine subscription offers, coupons, food samples, investment opportunities, and the like. This is five times the amount of junk mail received by consumers in any other country. More than half of all adults in the United States purchase something by mail every year, and millions of them are victims of mail fraud.

Mail fraud, according to the 1872 Postal Service Law, is the use of the mails for "any scheme to defraud, or for obtaining money or property by means of false or fraudulent pretenses." Mail fraud is one of the top five areas of consumer complaints to government agencies.

Mail frauds work because people frequently do not recognize them as deceitful until it is too late. Some people are victims because of that common human weakness, an inability to resist an apparent bargain. Others are victimized because they lack knowledge. Deceptive mail-order schemes often appear to be a good deal, an excellent business opportunity, or a chance to make a quick buck. To avoid mail fraud, the consumer has to know it when he or she sees it. The most familiar tactic in mail fraud is misleading or false advertisements by which the perpetrators use the mails to lure consumers into their scams. Consumers are led to believe that they are getting a really good deal, perhaps something free. The consumer unwittingly puts up money expecting a product of excellent quality, but instead receives something of poor quality and of little or no value.

Lack of physical contact with victims makes identification of mail-order crooks difficult. Also, the geographic distance between the victim and the perpetrators makes apprehension more difficult and expensive. Because of the usual small amount of money that is lost, many consumers are willing to chalk up the loss to experience rather than report it to authorities. Still, the U.S. Postal Service manages to obtain convictions against about 1000 swindlers each year.

Telemarketing to Get Your Money

The U.S. Office of Consumer Affairs reports that over 300,000 solicitors working for over 30,000 businesses telephone more than 18 million Americans every day. According to the Federal Trade Commission, telemarketers focus about two thirds of their calls on the elderly and the general public; they also target investors and small business owners. The most popular telemarketing frauds are travel packages, awards and other "prizes," sale of water treatment units, and charitable solicitations (also known as **telefunding**). Telemarketing continues to be one of the top five areas of consumer complaints to government agencies.

Telemarketing is selling a product or service over the telephone. Many worthwhile products are marketed using telecommunications, such as up-to-date financial news, stock quotations, insurance company financial-soundness ratings, legal aid by the minute, sample music cuts, and critiques of latest films.

At the same time, almost anything can be sold by unscrupulous sellers over the telephone, including bad deals on prize offers, penny stocks, office supplies, magazine subscriptions, credit repair, job opportunities, precious metals, travel packages, art, business ventures, cellular telephone lotteries, travel clubs, coupon books, and fake charities. The term **telefrauds** describes what unscrupulous telephone salespeople do—use the telephone for non-legitimate sales. Many people describe the proliferation of legitimate and unscrupulous telemarketing techniques as **junk calls**.

Both good and bad telemarketing sellers use 800-numbers and 900-numbers to market goods and services. An **800-number** is a toll-free long-distance telephone line; **888-numbers** now are also toll-free. About 40 percent of all long-distance calls are made to 800-numbers. A **900-number** is a caller-paid long distance service that allow consumers and businesses to access information over the telephone. (Local callers dial **976-numbers** the same way.) The caller pays for telephone numbers with 900 and 976 prefixes. Watch out when responding to advertisements that give an area code that seems unfamiliar because it may be an international number that is long-distance, and the toll charges may not be enormous.

One indicted telemarketing promoter was quoted as saying that, "If you ask 100 people any question, at least 3 of them will say yes. With the right pitch, you can sell anything over the telephone." The American Association of Retired Persons estimates that telephone marketing swindlers cheat American consumers out of $40 billion annually. The North American Securities Association reports that consumers lose $1 million an hour to investment scams promoted over the telephone. Senator Richard H. Bryan says that the concept of "reach out and cheat someone" clearly applies to the telemarketing industry.

Many telemarketing scams originate out of **boiler rooms**. This is a place (historically in the basement next to the heating unit) where a number of people use high-pressure telephone sales tactics to sell stock, commodities, petroleum partnerships, unmined gold, re-opened oil wells, land, travel clubs, and other so-called opportunities. The National Fraud Information Center (800-876-7060), coordinated by the National Consumers League, can advise you with information, referral services and assistance should you have questions. One popular telemarketing prize is a "$100 savings certificate," that, rather than being a U.S. Government Series EE savings bond, is a "savings coupon" good towards the purchase of merchandise from a small catalog of overpriced goods.

Prizes and Free Gifts

Nearly all consumers in the United States have received (and probably will again in the future) at least one official-looking "notice" or telephone call stating that they are the "guaranteed winner" of one of the following six prizes worth thousands of dollars, including a glamorous vacation or a new automobile. Such claims are rarely true. Prizes and free gifts offered by sellers are simply come-ons. Such sellers simply want to interest consumers in something. Legitimate businesses use these marketing techniques because they work; so do unscrupulous sellers.

Prizes are a popular way to interest consumers into buying home fire-prevention systems, raw land for investment purposes, vacation condominium time shares, home security systems, water treatment systems, vitamins, and a host of other products they are not likely to buy without some persuasive encouragement. Selling such products recovers the promoter's money spent giving away the cheap prizes. (You don't really think any legitimate business can give away a camera worth $149, do you?) Yes, manufacturers can make a 35-mm camera for $5, and semiprecious stones can be put into a setting for $3. Such products are truly cheap, but laws do not require that good-quality prizes must be given away. The truth is that you always win the cheapest prize.

Gifts and prizes are used to get consumers to the telephone or into the showroom so the persuasive sales force can interest them in overpriced products and services. The values of the prizes, such as jewelry, are grossly misrepresented. Discount coupons, for example, instead of being usable at stores on "Mainstreet America," may only be utilized at facilities of the sponsor of the prize promotion.

One of the gambits commonly used by scam telemarketing operators is the guise of marketing research in combination with prizes and awards. The promoters ask you to help their market research by testing a product. To encourage participation, consumers are offered fabulous gifts and prizes with inflated values, either free or at substantial discounts, such as a motor boat or a motorcycle. To receive the merchandise, the consumer must send in a "redemption fee" or pay a "shipping-tax-and-handling fee", perhaps $295 to $495. It turns out that the fee is much higher than the value of the product.

Sweepstakes

A **sweepstakes** is an advertising or promotional device by which prizes are awarded to participating consumers by chance, with no purchase or entry-fee required in order to win. One's chances of winning are determined by the number of participants and the number of prizes to be awarded. Some sweepstakes sponsors, especially those who are marketing products and services, put up all the prize money themselves. Marketers-both legitimate and fraudulent-use sweepstakes because they are extremely effective in generating attention for the sponsoring companies. People should *never* have to order something or pay a fee to enter and win a sweepstakes.

In contrast to a sweepstakes, a **lottery** is a promotional device by which prizes are awarded to members of the public by chance but which requires some form of payment in order to participate. Here the participants' contributions form a fund to be awarded as a prize to the winner or winners. Only states and certain exempt charitable organizations may conduct lotteries; all other lotteries are illegal.

The highly publicized sweepstakes by Publisher's Clearinghouse, Reader's Digest, and American Family Publishers are legitimate, and they also sell lots of magazines. These reputable companies sell magazine subscriptions through direct mail, and a proven way of getting people to return their forms is to run a sweepstakes. Millions enter the contest and some also order magazines. By the way, being named a "finalist" means that you sent in a previous entry; it does not improve your odds. By law, competitors in sweepstakes competitions must have an equal chance of winning. This means, for example, regardless of whether or not you purchased magazines through a Publisher's Clearinghouse offer. Also, a sweepstakes sponsor must disclose the odds of winning.

These well-known companies do give away all the prizes, although you probably will not win. Publisher's Clearinghouse odds are typical; the chances of winning $1000 to $60,000 are 1 in 122.5 million; you have 1 chance in 12.5 million of winning $500, 1 chance in 4.9 million of winning $100, 1 chance in 2.45 million of winning $50, and 1 chance in 2869 of winning $5. Columbia University statistics professor Herbert Robbins calculated the odds. Comedian David Letterman once accurately joked that, "the odds of winning Publisher's Clearinghouse are about the same as not entering at all."

Some fraudulent operators have been calling consumers telling them that they have won the Reader's Digest Sweepstakes, or another sweepstakes. Then they say that the winnings may not be released until a cash or certified check in the amount of $500, or even $10,000, was sent by overnight courier or wire service to cover shipping, handling, and taxes. The bad guys even send a courier service to the conned consumer's home to pick up the money, which will never be seen again.

A variation of the fraudulent sweepstakes occurs when the winners (or should that be "losers"?) are invited to join a sweepstakes club, perhaps for only $5 a month. The "winners" are promised that the company will use its "special formula" to identify the sweepstakes-that are held monthly-that offer them the greatest odds of winning; then the company signs them up. Victims-often the elderly-are later talked into joining a number of similar clubs. Losses of $1000 to $3000-a month!-are common. Recently, a scam artist had his 42 sweepstakes companies closed by the federal government, but not before he grossed $82 million in just one year.

Contests

A variety of companies offer premiums and prizes to promote their products to consumers. Such contests are often confused with sweepstakes. Postcards and other mailings are usually used which offer "congratulations" to you as the winner of some prize.

Many contests purposely have very easy, simple solutions. Once the consumer mails in his or her solution, he or she is sent a prize for winning, although it is usually something of low quality and of little value.

Some sewing machine and vacuum machine manufacturers, for example, encourage potential buyers with prizes. They award books, cameras, and jewelry to winners of "easy-to win" or "everybody-really-wins" contests. To claim a prize, a consumer need only respond correctly to the promoter's question(s), mail in some postal card response, telephone the seller, or visit the sales showroom.

Some telemarketers, but especially the unscrupulous ones, use 900-numbers to market contest offers and sweepstake-like promotions. You, the "lucky winner", might also be told that you are eligible to enter a **tie-breaker contest** where, for an additional fee, you are allowed to compete for a much larger prize. Such telemarketers typically offer a *series* of tie-breaker contests, offering the hope of winning some grand prize. Of course, there is no big prize; but there are huge 900-number bills instead.

Some contest scams require that as a winner all you have to do is to telephone the company's 900-number to collect the prize. Using 900-numbers costs the calling consumer lots of money, often $15 to $60 to simply call up and ask about the prize. To entice people to respond, slick telemarketers sometimes allow victims to call toll-free 800-numbers where they get a recording saying that in order to receive the prize they must call another number, and yes, it is a 900-number.

Other fraudulent contests require that the "winner" pay money up front, often several hundred dollars, to collect the award. Still other scams require that you call a 900-number to "verify", "redeem", or "audit" the existence of your prize. If paid, such verification, redemption, and auditing fees will never be seen again. Such is also the case with the payment of "refundable deposits" and "pre-payment of taxes". The price of the call to find out what you have "won" could be $35, $50, or $149. You pay for the call but typically receive nothing. Or, you may be asked to pay a $49 or $299 "shipping and handling fee", perhaps for a fishing boat and later you receive a toy boat.

Yet another variation of the contest scam occurs when one calls to say that "as a credit card holder you have won." The caller then asks for your credit card number for "verification" purposes. If you do give them your number, your next month's credit card bill is likely to reveal substantial unauthorized charges to your account.

Postcards Saying, "You Definitely Have Won!"

A postcard addressed to you might say, "One of the individuals named below [your name is listed] ... is a guaranteed winner of a $1000 certified check," "A Mercedes-Benz Sedan," or "A Hawaiian vacation for two." Others say, "You are one of the first round prize winners in the $5000 Instant Cash Sweepstakes," "You have a one in three chance of winning a third-round prize of $1000," "You have definitely won!" a motor vehicle, a color TV, $10,000 in cash, a dream vacation, a car telephone, or something else. Others ask you to call a telephone number with a 900 area code, where the toll charges can be as much as the company wishes-sometimes $50 or more.

Some telemarketers ask you to call a toll-free 800-number, where you are subject to persuasive suggestions to part with a little time or money, or both. Some companies ask that you only return the postcard indicating your interest; others ask that you enclose a few dollars. The intent is to get the consumer's interest and then sell magazines, cosmetics, an investment opportunity, or another special deal. As disclosed in small print (and sometimes not disclosed at all because they are lying), most entrants will get the minimum prize, inevitably something worth $10 or less. Also, if you mistakenly provide the telemarketers with your credit card number-perhaps as part of the verification process-they are likely to place unauthorized charges on your credit account. Many of these companies also make money selling the names of **sales leads**—those who answer the mailings—to other businesses which may or may not be legitimate.

Many Charities Are Not What They Claim To Be

About 7 in 10 American households make charitable donations each year, averaging $800 a year. However, the generous American public winds up giving part of that money—actually billions of dollars annually—to fraudulent charities too. Many disreputable companies use a variation of the name of a nationally recognized charity so they sound like credible organizations. When you are considering giving money and you want to avoid unscrupulous organizations, you must learn how to spot fraudulent charity appeals and obtain adequate information about how the charitable group plans to spend your donation. You need to be confident that most of your contribution is going to the charity's programs, not being spent on fundraising and administrative costs (including high salaries for officers).

Americans are a giving people, and unscrupulous charitable solicitation promoters are aware of this fact. Some charities play on feelings of guilt: "Won't you contribute to the starving Africans?" Others just want a token amount because you can afford it: "Won't you contribute just $5 to help?" Often the credentials of such organizations seem

> **CONSUMER UPDATE:**
> **The Gifts and Prizes ... What They Really Are**
>
> Sellers try hard to convince consumers that the "prize" they have won is worth a lot of money. Consumers are enticed to "send money for shipping and handling" or "come and listen to a one-hour sales presentation with no obligation." In actuality, the prizes and gifts are simply worthless.
>
> - "1/2 Carat Diamond Ring" ... A zirconia stone valued at $10
> - "1 Carat Genuine Semi-precious Store" ... A cheap gemstone valued at $3
> - "Big Screen Television" ... A big-screen projection system that reflects a fuzzy picture from your TV screen that is enlarged against a wall, valued at $10
> - "$500 Savings Bond" ... A zero-coupon bond of a corporation currently valued at $5 because the company is near bankruptcy and won't be around 30 years later to pay the $500
> - "35 Millimeter Camera" ... An all-plastic camera worth about the price of a roll of film
> - "Genuine Leather-Like Luggage" ... A cheap plastic bag shaped like luggage with metal brackets so weak that they would collapse if a child sat on it
> - "Vacation cruise" ... You must send in a redemption fee of $295
> - "Motorcycle" ... A plastic replica suitable for a small child
> - "Full-size Motor Boat" ... A five-foot inflatable rubber raft powered by a small battery-activated motor
>
> *Carol Ann Walker, Personal Finance Manager/Air Force Aid Officer, Peterson Air Force Base, Colorado

legitimate and their names sound familiar. Consumers rarely find out that they have given to a fake charity. All statements and documentation deserve close attention, particularly when the charities are not well known to the consumer. There are outright fraudulent charitable groups preying on the generosity of the American people.

There also are charities that might better be called **quasi-charities**. These are charities that have not yet been closed down by a government agency, but they appear to be unscrupulous, in part because they spend an excessively high proportion of their income on administrative expenses and fund raising and they give very little money to those really in need. Any charity that spends more than 25 cents out of every dollar of income on fund-raising and administrative expenses is suspect.

The major activity of most such quasi-charities is "program services" for public education about cancer, heart disease, orphaned animals, or whatever. They "educate" the public by mailing out additional solicitation letters. That, plus mailing costs, fat salaries, and overhead, eats up most of the money raised. They are greedy, self-serving operations. The executive director of one Better Business Bureau states that, "It happens all the time, and unfortunately, there's not much that the law can do."

Legitimate charities sometimes pay exorbitant fees to professional fund raisers-commercial telemarketers-to collect for them. The fees are often as high as 80 percent. For example, in a recent year the Marketing Corporation of America raised over $12 million for the March of Dimes, although less than half went to the charity. Reese Brothers raised $2.3 million for Mothers Against Drunk Driving (MADD), but the charity only received $1.2 million. Many commercial telemarketers contract with charities to pay them a flat fee (perhaps $25,000) to use their name for 12 weeks of solicitations during which time they might collect $400,000. Recently it was disclosed that the Marine Toys for Tots Foundation, the fundraising organization for the Marine's Christmas drive, had collected $10 million the previous two years and spent nothing on toys. To be certain that your money goes to the charity and not a fund-raising firm, send your check directly to the charity.

It is appropriate for you to ask for a written disclosure of the percentage of your money that will actually be delivered to the primary charitable cause. At least 50 or 60 percent of each dollar ought to go towards the main mission of the charity. Get the disclosure in writing because some telemarketing charities simply lie telling people that "100 percent of the proceeds go to the XYZ charity," when in fact proceeds means "money after expenses."

Some charities use contests to attract donors in which the participants' contributions create a fund to be awarded as prizes to the winners. The promoters describe the charitable programs, explain the contest game along with the rules and regulations, and ask that the contestant return the entry form with or without a donation. Many generous people send in donations.

By necessity, charities have full-time fund-raising specialists who either write, telephone, or knock on the household doors of consumers. Some charities employ outside specialists under contract to raise funds. Toiletries, brooms, candy, and household products are the types of things sold by private companies to consumers on behalf of charitable organizations. Too often the charity benefits very little through such collections.

Recent data from the Philanthropic Advisory Service of the Council of Better Business Bureaus reveal the ten most-asked-about national charities that have the highest fund raising expenses: Vietnow, National Caregiving Foundation, Oblate Missions, Walker Cancer Research Center, Help Hospitalized Veterans, Dakota Indian Foundation, Cancer Fund of America, Retired Enlisted Association, North Shore Animal League, and Marine Toys for Tots Foundation.

The question to ask is how much of every dollar collected goes to those for whom it is collected. To check the legitimacy of a charitable organization contact: (1) a local Better Business Bureau, or (2) the state Office of Consumer Affairs. These groups also can provide addresses of charities to which letters can be sent by consumers seeking financial details.

Two watchdog groups can provide free written reports on fund-raising costs for national charities: (1) The Philanthropic Advisory Service of the Council of Better Business Bureaus (4200 Wilson Blvd., Arlington, VA 22203-1804/703-276-0100), and (2) National Charities Information Bureau (19 Union Square West, Dept. FT, New York, NY 10003-3395/212-929-6300). Every charitable organization ought to be willing to provide an annual report on request that describes its purpose, programs, accomplishments, and some financial details. The Council of Better Business Bureaus publishes a *Annual Charity Index* paperback guide that provides snapshots of over 200 of the most-asked-about charities.

Chapter 4

Buying Ripoffs and Scams

Numerous misrepresentations and scams exist to take advantage of consumers who are enticed to spend money trying to improve the efficiency of their buying practices. These ripoffs and scams prey upon people who are consciously trying to buy products and services at low or fair prices. Popular ripoffs include buying clubs, rent-to-own, coupon books, vacation certificates, vacation travel clubs, tour operators, scholarship aid, secured credit cards, credit repair clinics, service contracts (also called "extended warranties"), financing for consumers with no or bad credit, home-related scams, and second mortgages. By cautiously looking for what is wrong with such deals you can avoid being victimized.

Buying Clubs

Buying-club promoters often use telephone solicitations to entice people to come to their offices. The sales office is usually a suite of motel rooms rented for a few weeks. Consumers are given gifts for being willing to "just listen to an explanation about our exciting membership buying program."

Most of these outfits are nationally based, and they come through communities that have nursing schools, vocational schools, and colleges. They like the concentrations of large numbers of people. Persuasive salespersons talk students and townspeople into signing contracts for $500 or more. For paying this amount, the consumer gets an upgraded gift, such as a stereo or television (which is not worth $500), a catalog showing all the goods available through the buying club (brand-name goods only, since Sears, Penney's, and others refuse to participate), and a toll-free telephone number for placing orders. Once the consumer has signed the contract, they are stuck.[1]

What happens is that you will have problems with high shipping costs, setup charges, nondelivery of merchandise, delays in shipping, unavailability of goods, substitution of goods for out-of-stock items, unavailability of the latest models, difficulties in returning goods, long-term contracts, firms going bankrupt, and warranty service. Many duped consumers plunk down their money failing to realize that they can get the same products for the same or better prices at local discount stores, or through reputable catalog mail-order buying services (such as Unity Buying Club or United Buying Service) that charge annual membership fees of $5 to $15. Not surprisingly, most buying clubs do not give out their price lists to consumers because it would allow comparison shopping in advance of joining.

Rent-to-Own

A rent-to-own contract is easy to contract to a standard credit contract. If a consumer buys a $400 television set on an 18-month credit contract, he or she might pay $27 a month, or $480 in total. Under an 18-month RTO plan, the consumer could pay $25 a month for many more months, perhaps totaling $1,200 for the same television. If rent-to-own payments were considered interest, the effective annual rate in this example would be over 200 percent. Renters who miss a payment may have their goods repossessed; to get them back, they have to begin renting again.

Rent-to-own (RTO) businesses exist so that consumers can obtain durable goods (including household goods and vehicles) using a series of short-term rental-purchase agreements. People respond to advertisements that say, "No credit hassle!", "No long-term commitment!", "No down payment!", and "Free service in your home!" There are no down payments or credit checks required. Such goods as televisions, stereos, microwave ovens, washers and dryers, video equipment, refrigerators, automobiles, and furniture can be obtained by making regular payments. This can eventually lead to ownership over a period of time. Each weekly or monthly payment creates a new rental

---

[1]Colorado allows purchasers of buying club contracts valued at $100 or more a one-day cooling-off period to rescind the contract. See Chapter 3 for advice on getting out of contracts.

> **CONSUMER UPDATE:**
> **Official Military Vendors Do *Not* Exist**
>
> Though they have the appearance of being "officially sanctioned", vendors located in the Navy, Post Exchange and in connected malls are just businesses that have paid for floor space. The only requirements to do business in these areas are that the businesses continue pay for the space in military malls and provide a recognized service to the military community. There are no criteria to assure "official" status and, therefore, legitimacy. Unless the products and advertising are proven illegal or contrary to good order and discipline, they may continue to operate and appeal to military consumers.
>
> *Dean Brassington, Navy Family Services Center, Norfolk, Virginia

agreement, with the customer having no obligation to continue beyond the present period.

Many RTOs charge exorbitant prices; they are located primarily in poor inner-city and rural areas. Twenty percent of the customers at the nation's largest rent-to-own company, Rent-A-Center, with 1000+ stores, are unemployed and receiving government aid. If you have a poor credit history or experience difficulty raising the amount of money needed for purchasing, the weekly or monthly payments may seem so low that the terms are attractive. Rent-to-own companies are aggressive collectors of past- due amounts and frequently repossess goods.

Rent-to-own businesses are exempt from the state and federal laws governing credit because they offer "rental lease" contracts instead of credit contracts, thus no credit has been extended. (Only the state of Pennsylvania defines rent-to-own as credit sales, and RTO interest rates there are limited to 18 percent.) RTOs also are usually exempt from provisions in the Uniform Commercial Code, usury laws, and cooling-off laws. Because the renter is making payments that add up to much more than the cost of an item, conceptually, the effect is the same as charging interest.

A California Public Interest Research Group study revealed that RTO contracts often have charges equivalent to 200 to 300 percent interest, instead of the more typical 16 to 24 percent for similar credit purchases in standard retail stores. Critics called this exploitation.

Coupon Books

You may think you are getting a good deal when you buy a book of coupons purporting to offer excellent values. With **coupon books**, the consumer is offered free merchandise or services or discounted prices on goods and services. The coupon book might cost $39.95 for six discounted restaurant meals in a community or $149.95 for several nights of lodging at various motels. Three problems exist: (1) the coupons often have restrictions as to times and locations which may not be convenient, (2) the coupon book promoters often sell many more than the participating merchants have been led to believe, and later the merchants may be unwilling to honor all the requests, and (3) some of these operations get a few businesses to agree to participate and then simply lie about the others. As the complaints start to come in, the promoter quickly leaves town to go elsewhere seeking more victims.

Vacation Certificates

Promoters of **vacation certificates** claim that for only $59.95 or perhaps $129.95, you are eligible for, "Three days and two nights of free lodging at excellent hotels in Las Vegas, Miami, New Orleans, or even Hawaii," or any number of other desirable vacation spots. Vacation certificates typically include discount or free coupons for a handful of hotels, selected restaurants, and certain attractions in a resort area. The deal is that you pay lots of dollars for something of very little value, and, because of certain reasons described below, it is likely that you will not be able to use the certificate anyhow. Many consumers, especially young people, falsely believe that these certificates have substantial value. The American Society of Travel Agents reports that of all the travel vouchers sold, only ten percent provided customers with actual vacations.

This scheme is sometimes tied into a legitimate promotion by a local supermarket or department store that is unaware of the minuscule value of the vacation certificates. The big prize winner might receive groceries while the other winners might receive vacation certificates.

To receive a free vacation certificate, you may be required to attend a sales presentation. Sometimes there are age or income conditions, or a requirement that you be accompanied by your spouse, so that you both will be there to sign on the dotted line of a contract.

The lure of a free vacation certificate is often used in advertising to draw people to the seller's sales sites with the goal of selling a specific product or service. Vacation certificates are used by time-share resorts, membership campgrounds, automobile dealers, and solar energy companies as prizes. Some vacation certificate promoters ask for a major credit-card number to validate a complimentary vacation and then illegally charge fees on the consumer's credit-card account.

Winners of vacation certificates sometimes are required to pay a non-refundable processing and handling fee, or a refundable deposit from $50 to $100 to reserve each vacation time request. And, of course, they say, "Yes, we can charge the amount to your credit card!" They promise that the deposit will be returned upon your arrival at the place of lodging or after the vacation is complete. It's not.

Telemarketers sell vacation certificates, too. Here the consumer pays a fee of $50 to $500 to receive a travel certificate that includes round-trip air transportation for one person and lodging for two people for a week in London, Hawaii, or another vacation spot. Once they have the money or credit card number, the victim discovers that oral misrepresentations occurred because they cannot deliver the promised deals. When written materials are sent describing the offer, the writing contradicts what was said on the telephone. (If it is the same, they simply may be lying.) Also, reservations are difficult to confirm, and you must comply with hard-to-meet hidden or expensive conditions. In spite of suggestions to the contrary, refunds do not exist.

Complaints about these deals include: the written information given after the sales presentation is different from what was promised, the available lodging is typically at cheap hotels that have names that sound like the better hotels, the hotel accommodations can only be obtained through the promoter, rooms are available only on a space-available basis, the hotel price is a daily rate based on occupancy of several days, airline reservations are almost impossible to obtain, the cost for the second airfare ticket is over $1000, there are substantial charges for extra fees, and the certificates are limited to use during off-season time periods, with perhaps 80 percent of the year being considered the peak season.

Chapter 4:   Buying Ripoffs and Scams   41

Also, such vacations are not free when you have to pay for part or all of the transportation, meals, drinks, taxes, and miscellaneous expenses. It is virtually impossible to get a refund from one of these promoters because most declare bankruptcy within a year of starting business.

Vacation Travel Clubs[2]

Vacation travel clubs are for-profit organizations that in return for an advance fee, usually over $100, grant a consumer the privilege to arrange or obtain future travel or travel facilities through or from the organization. In essence, these are travel services agreements.

Today's vacation club operators ask consumers to buy "points" that theoretically may be used to enjoy weeks in a variety of accommodations at different sites throughout the year. Those who purchase the minimum number of points may use the tiny cubicle of a room during the worst season; those who buy of lot of points can have weeks of luxury at almost any of the finest resorts in the world during the best times of the year.

If you pay the $8,000 purchase price in cash, the daily rate for the vacation room might be less than $90. Most vacation travel club buyers, however, put up only the minimum 20 percent down payment and finance the balance. Adding in maintenance costs pushes the average daily rate for the financed vacation club deal to over $110. Most of the dangers of real estate timeshares (see Chapter 10) accompany vacation travel clubs, such as rising maintenance fees, special assessments for renovations, and the virtual impossibility of selling the vacation club rights to someone else.

Tour Operators

After putting down $5,000 for a tour of several Asian countries, it was sad for Herta Fletcher to discover a few days before her scheduled departure that her certified check had been cashed and that the tour operator had declared bankruptcy.[3] Legal fees could run $5,000 to get her money back. This type of story is almost commonplace today because there is no federal or state regulation of tour operators or travel agents. Hundreds and hundreds of travelers are stranded every year; some are students, some are military personnel.

Of over 350 national selling tour operators, about 50 do the majority of the business. Only 35 of those are members of the U.S. Tour Operators Association (USTOA), and four have declared bankruptcy in the past three years. USTOA has a consumer protection plan for member-sold tours so people with tickets from companies that fail get their money back. Concerned consumers should be certain that their tour operator has a current bond with USTOA; telephone 212-750-7371. A different trade association, National Tour Association (800-682-8886) offers limited protection. Wise consumers always put the cost of a tour on their credit card, so they have the right to not pay the bill for 60 days from the date of the charges should the trip fall through. (See Chapter

---

[2]Some of the information for this section was obtained from *Money* magazine, October 1994, pages 33-34.

[3]Details for some of this section were obtained from Lynn Woods, Travel Tales From Hell, *Kiplinger's Personal Finance Magazine*, April, 1994, 121-126.

10 for details.) Another form of protection is to purchase **trip cancellation and interruption insurance** coverage from a third-party, not a policy from the tour operator.

Scholarship Aid

It seems that during times of rising tuition bills, the **scholarship aid** businesses come out of the cracks in the sewer. Advertisements are placed in school newspapers suggesting: "We match at least two scholarships to your abilities!" "Money for college, results guaranteed!" "Scholarships go begging every year because people do not apply!" Many students have received postcards in the mail, perhaps from something called the "National Scholarship Foundation", promising a guaranteed scholarship because of the student's "present academic and financial circumstances". Perhaps saddest of all because these students rarely can afford to waste money, are advertisements which claim, "Guaranteed scholarships for foreign students!"

Tens of thousands of students every year fall for such misrepresentations. How nice it would be if the claims were true, but they are not! The "unclaimed billions" in the advertisements count employee tuition benefits and the money given out in federal grants. Contrary to advertised promises, even the best of these services offer only leads, not money. For the fee of $45, $119 or even $495, the consumer-applicant receives a computer listing of scholarships that are available as of a certain date (when the information was compiled by the promoters). This is nearly useless information. Common experiences include inappropriate leads, application deadlines that have passed, wrong addresses, incorrect telephone numbers, and strict eligibility requirements.

Spending three or four hours with a high school guidance counselor or a college financial aid officer looking through the school's library of scholarship materials will locate many more and much better quality leads for funds. Also, look in the library for *The College Money Handbook* (Peterson's Guides), *Paying Less for College* (Peterson's), and Robert and Ann Leider's *Don't Miss Out* (Octameron Press). Most commercial scholarship businesses are ripoffs. The worst firms file for bankruptcy; the "best" continue to sell something of little value.

Secured Credit Cards

Some consumers are ineligible to receive a major credit card from a traditional lending organization because of insufficient income, an old bankruptcy, minimal credit history, a recent divorce, or a past credit delinquency even though that problem has been resolved. Advertisements from companies offering **secured credit cards** often are found in the classified sections of newspapers and magazines. Here banks offer to people with a poor credit rating (or none whatsoever) who meet some requirements and have no or few outstanding debts. Banks promise to assist in establishing or improving a person's credit rating within a year by offering Visa or MasterCard credit cards in exchange for cash collateral.

> **CONSUMER UPDATE:**
> **Encyclopedia Sales Contracts that "Cannot" be Canceled**
>
> A persistent and overly ambitious encyclopedia salesperson obtains a list of the new couples that have moved to a particular locale. After persuading the people to purchase the set of encyclopedias, he has them sign one additional document-a one sentence letter that says, "Due to the time and costs associated with the processing of your order, your account is billed the amount of $85, and this fee is waived for all completed contracts; however, the fee remains valid if you cancel the contract within three business days after it is signed."
>
> Such a "contract" is unbelievable! It is also illegal and unenforceable in a court of law.
>
> Unfortunately, many encyclopedia buyers believe such illegal letter contracts and are afraid to exercise their legitimate right to cancel such contracts. Under federal law, contracts signed in one's home may be canceled within three business days when the home is used as security for the loan. Also, under the Federal Trade Commission's Door-to-Door Sales regulation (also known as a **cooling-off period law**), sales agreements made for $25 or more anywhere except the seller's normal place of business may be canceled by the consumer within three business days of the purchase. State laws typically provide additional cooling-off rights.
>
> *Tom Snyder, Financial Counselor, Hurlburt Field, Florida

The bank requires a deposit of $500 or $1000 and that amount provides the consumer with a credit limit of as little as $300. Typically, the deposit earns only 3 percent while finance charges on unpaid balances run as high as 24 percent. Banks often tack on substantial amounts for application fees, annual dues, late-payment fees, and charges for exceeding the credit limit. What remains crucial for consumers is that the secured credit card company report information to credit bureaus that may later help get them an improved credit rating and access to regular credit cards. A positive aspect of secured credit cards is that they allow uncreditworthy consumers to prove their worthiness so that they can move up to a regular, unsecured card.[4]

Credit Repair Clinics that Promise to Erase Bad Information

Beware of so-called **credit repair clinics**, credit service companies, or "credit doctors" because they simply lie to consumers. Unscrupulous operations are easy to spot because they make unrealistic promises that, for a fee of $500, $1000, or even more, you will not be turned down for credit ever again. They promise that they can clean up a consumer's credit report. Some credit repair clinics even promise to provide consumers

---

[4]Consumer Action, a San Francisco consumer organization, offers a free list of institutions nationally that offer low-cost secured credit cards, which can be obtained by sending a self-addressed stamped envelope to 116 New Montgomery Street, Suite 223, San Francisco, CA 94105.

with a new credit history;[5] others promise to establish credit for a person who has none. They promise to remove adverse information, such as records of late payments or collection actions, from a consumer's files.

The reality is that good and bad information generally remains in your credit file for no more than 7 years, or 10 years for personal bankruptcy. The credit repair clinics promise to refund their fee if all is not accomplished. That is a false statement, too.

The premise of this scheme is that the organization invokes on the consumer's behalf provisions of the Fair Credit Reporting Act that allow consumers to protest items in their credit file, which is something consumers can do themselves at little or no cost if they wish. (See Chapter 10.) Since a credit bureau is required to verify all disputed items within a reasonable time (usually 30 days) or else delete it, the credit repair company floods the credit bureau with challenges. The hope is that a number of items will not be verified and as a result, be temporarily dropped from the file, creating a "window of opportunity" for clients to borrow. The repair is at best temporary because once a credit bureau has verified an item, even if it is a month later, the information goes right back into the credit bureau file. If negative information is eliminated, it is likely to be reinstated when old lenders file new reports with credit bureaus.

Consumers should know that if they have a bad credit record it cannot be changed. Further, if there is a mistake in your credit file, you can get it off your record yourself by contacting the local credit bureau that has your file. Most of these credit repair clinics go out of business within 6 months or a year as consumer complaints mount. They don't give refunds. They try to stay ahead of the authorities, who frequently charge them with deceptive advertising. The FTC says that these companies "do not improve the credit histories of the vast majority of clients." Over twenty-five states have adopted legislation to regulate credit repair clinics.

These firms should not be confused with legitimate consumer credit counseling service (CCCS) organizations, which may charge nothing, or as little as $15, for 1 or 2 hours of credit and budget counseling advice.[6]

Service Contracts—Not Worth the Money

A **service contract** (**maintenance agreement** or **extended warranty**) is an agreement separate from and not part of the basis of a sale of products and services to make repairs on defective or malfunctioning products. A service contract is an agreement between the buyer of a product and the contract seller (a dealer, manufacturer, or independent insurance company), to whom the buyer has paid a fee, to provide free or nearly free maintenance or repair (or both) to certain components of the product for some specified time period. A service contract is purchased separately from the purchase of the product,

---

[5]People who attempt to create a new identity so they can request a new and clean credit history are sometimes unwisely advised (with the advice of a credit repair clinic) to request an **employer identification number (EIN)** from the Internal Revenue Service, using a different address (such as that of a friend), to use on credit applications. Such an effort is illegal on several federal grounds: lying to the IRS, misusing a Social Security number, lying to a bank or other creditor, and mail fraud.

[6]A local CCCS office can be located by writing the National Foundation for Consumer Credit, 8701 Georgia Avenue, Suite 507, Silver Spring, MD 20910, or telephoning 301-589-5600 or 800-388-2227. The services are provided at little or no cost to those seeking assistance. Nonprofit counseling assistance also can be obtained from the 60 member agencies of Family Service America (FSA); direct inquires to FSA, 11700 West Lake Park Drive, Milwaukee, WI 53224.

> **CONSUMER UPDATE:**
> **Free Rides for Military Personnel**
>
> Many military personnel do not own private vehicles, so when they are offered a free ride from a shopping center back to their base, they often accept. Some vehicles are specially marked "Courtesy vans for active-duty personnel." The hucksters ask military passersby if they would like the opportunity to win a motorcycle or other prize. They may offer six free rides back to base for listening to one sales presentation. Typically, attractive women drive the vans, make the sales pitch, and transport the victims to the company office where high-pressure salespersons persuade them to sign contracts to purchase overpriced camera and film packages, stereo equipment, or other goods, often for $700, $1000 or more, plus interest.

often automobiles, electronics, and appliances.

Nearly two-thirds of all consumer electronics products are sold with service contracts, even though it makes little economic sense to insure against risks that can, if necessary, be paid for out of current income or savings. This occurs despite the fact that executives in industries where such contracts are sold agree that the products that are being sold today are the most reliable they have ever been. James J. Jodl explains in *Appliance Service News*, for example, that, "If you don't have a problem within the first three to six months, chances are you won't have one for another 12 years."

The cost of a service contract is usually between 10 and 50 percent of the price of the item purchased. The cost of a service contract typically is either paid in a lump sum or may require monthly payments by the purchaser. For example, a 25-inch television selling for $700 could have a service contract that promises to fix anything free, including parts and labor, for the first two years of ownership after the warranty expires. Such a contract could cost $72 a year, or $6 a month. On a new or almost new automobile, the cost could amount to $700 or more for a 3-year service contract.

Service contracts are almost pure profit, and that is why they are "sold" to consumers by salespersons. William Sliney, president of the Service Contract Industry Council, reports that profit margins for dealers are fantastic. For every $100 service contract sold, the retail store keeps $80 to $96. Service contracts are commonly called "extended warranties", even though they are purchase contracts and not warranties. Warranties are included in the price of a product, while the price of service contracts is normally added to the purchase price.

Service contracts are a form of insurance and are marketed in much the same manner. Before buying a service contract, consumers should first check the terms of the warranty since service contracts often duplicate a product's warranty coverage. It is important to recognize that service contracts do not offer the same legal rights as warranties.

Service contracts allow consumers to prepay for any service required. Based on massive amounts of repair information, the sellers of service contracts determine with great precision how many repairs each product will need in the future. Reliable products are not likely to need repair during the warranty period. For example, Component Guard, a large service-contract company, states that only 7 percent of the 45 million VCRs need servicing in the first year of ownership—when they are still under warranty! The president of Professional Servicers Association observes that fewer than 3 percent of electronic goods fail during an extended warranty period.

Stores make so much money selling service contracts that they often make more on the service contracts than on the products themselves. Service contracts are so profitable that sellers often telephone consumers about the time the manufacturer's warranty is up suggesting that an extended service contract be purchased.

One interesting service contract is offered by the American Express Company. It is offered solely to American Express cardholders at no additional cost above the annual membership fee. The plan has two parts: (1) a *purchase protection plan* that provides up to $50,000 in insurance coverage for card purchases against loss, theft, or accidental damage for 90 days from the date of purchase (the coverage is in excess of other applicable homeowner's or automobile insurance coverage of the cardholder), and (2) a *buyer's assurance protection plan* that doubles the free repair period of a manufacturer's warranty automatically, up to an extra year, on virtually all card purchases in the United States with manufacturer's warranties of five years or less (except motorized vehicles). Similar service contracts are being offered by other credit card companies, and even by some banks on checking accounts. The terms of such deals can be changed at any time. If these service contracts can be offered to consumers for "free", you can bet the real cost is not very much.

According to a *Wall Street Journal* article, court documents reveal that a typical Nissan automobile extended service warranty cost the consumer $795. Of that amount, $131 goes for insurance coverage that actually pays for repairs under the contract, Nissan gets $60, the warranty company gets $38, and $11 goes for membership in an automobile club. The remaining $555 goes to the dealer. That is a 70 percent profit ($555 - $795) earned on taking the few minutes persuading the customer and sending the signed contract to the insurance company. On the other hand, if you are the kind of person a "black cloud" of bad luck seems to hang over where unfortunate things happen to you often, a service contract might be an excellent purchase.

There are two times when one might consider a service contract: (1) If you are buying an expensive used vehicle with lots of optional electronic gizmos that might fail during the next twelve months, and (2) if you know that you have had a "black cloud" of bad luck following you all your life. Otherwise, service contracts are a ripoff offering consumers very little for their money. Also, you should know that because product manufacturers are aware of their obligations under implied warranty laws, many will repair merchandise past the warranty period free of charge, especially for consumers who are aggressive when complaining.

Financing for Consumers with No or Bad Credit

The classified advertisements of many newspapers and magazines are full of ads saying, "Bad credit, no problem," "Easy credit here," "All drivers can finance an auto here," and "Loans for everyone." People with no credit history and those who have blemishes on their credit records (perhaps because of a bankruptcy within the past ten years, some missed credit repayments on previous loans, or a few late utility bills) often do have difficulty obtaining credit for seemingly necessary purchases, i.e., automobile, television, washing machine.

Some lenders-**credit brokers**-specialize in preying on people who are experiencing difficulty in obtaining credit. Perhaps the borrower's credit record is a bit tarnished, maybe they never have had credit. The credit broker promises, for an advance fee of perhaps $500, to locate a source of credit for your needs and to obtain both a low interest rate and reasonable repayment terms. This sales pitch may sound good to a person desperate to pay for a major auto repair, an appliance breakdown or some other necessary expense. At best, the credit broker takes the fee and refers the needy borrower to high-interest loan companies; at worst, the broker takes the fee and disappears.

In addition, the credit contracts typically offered have onerous credit terms-interest rates that are extremely high, often in excess of 22 percent. Comparable lending rates for average credit customers might be 12 to 14 percent from banks and credit unions. While such lenders do play a vital role in society by providing credit to this segment of society, not all consumers who "think" they are bad credit risks, in fact, are, and they should aggressively try and get financing elsewhere. After being turned down for a loan at a credit union, for example, smart consumers take care to maintain an excellent credit repayment record for the following six months and then reapply. Such borrowers often are accepted for loans.

Home-Related Scams

The area of home sales and repairs continues to be the number one area of consumer complaints to government agencies. Virtually all the classic techniques of fraud are practiced against homeowners. Telemarketers often sell siding, roofing and storm windows to people at ripoff prices. Crooked salespeople arrive at homeowner's doors saying that, "I've just finished a driveway paving job (or painting, chimney repair, porch repair, whatever) down the street, and because of left-over materials I can give you a 'fantastic price.'" Other unscrupulous people knock on doors claiming to be "official inspectors" who need to examine the homeowner's furnace (plumbing, water heater, whatever); then they scare the consumer into making expensive, often unnecessary and poor quality repairs. Homeowners should be skeptical about all sellers who contact them in person or on the telephone, and they should follow the cautionary suggestions offered in Chapter 1 about how to avoid becoming a victim of fraud.

Second Mortgage Scam Against Homeowners

This scam affects limited-income older consumers, who either already own their homes or owe very little on the original mortgage. The shysters come by noticing perhaps that the roof needs repair or that the house could use some new siding. After making the often shoddy or incomplete home improvements, typically after charging excessively high fees to process the loan application and having the homeowner sign a financing agreement for an exorbitantly high 25 to 30 percent interest, the loans (called **second mortgages**), which are secured by a second mortgage on the property, are sold to other financial institutions (often the large, respectable banks in town). After the homeowner quickly fell behind making the high repayments, the financial institution would foreclose. The results: the homeowner gets thrown out on the street, the bank collects the debt owed, and the homeowner receives any excess money (usually not much) from the sale of the home. The American Association of Retired Persons conducted a 45-city survey and found that during a recent six-month period over 40,000 homeowners were affected.

Chapter 5

Vehicle Sales and Repairs

Part of the difficulties faced by consumers in the area of automobiles comes from the fact that the American automobile industry is one of the last bastions of **hard selling**, where the customer must be "sold" something by highly persuasive practices. Sometimes these techniques border on misrepresentation. Thus, it is no surprise that new and used car sales are one of the top five areas of consumer complaints to government agencies. The world of auto sales and repairs remains a market dominated by an attitude of **caveat emptor**—Let the buyer beware! This chapter focuses on fictitious list prices, high-balling the value of the trade-in allowance, low-balling the price of a new vehicle, and automobile repairs.

Fictitious List Prices

A **list price** is the posted amount that consumers are expected to pay for a product or service, and it is often the price suggested by the manufacturer. A truthful list price is found when substantial sales are actually made at that price in a particular market area. A list price on a product in a department store is usually truthful, since it is the actual price that people pay for the product. The list price on the window of a new car in a dealer showroom is pure imagery. Such prices are designed to make consumers believe they are saving money when they purchase an automobile for less than the list price. In fact, only about 3 percent of new car sales are made at list price.

Many used-car dealers also post less-than-truthful list prices and then give all customers a discount. A number of states and localities have regulations prohibiting the deceptive practice of false list prices, but it is difficult and expensive for governmental consumer protection agencies to conduct the in-depth investigations necessary to get enough evidence for conviction.

CONSUMER UPDATE:
Subleasing Someone Else's Vehicle is Risky Business

Some consumers fall for the dangerously expensive subleasing scam. Here a subleasing broker offers to arrange, for a fee, for you to sublease someone else's vehicle. You are supposed to take over the actual owner's loan or lease payments on their vehicle. These contracts are illegal in most states, and they typically violate the terms of the original loan or lease. This means that the lender can repossess the vehicle even after you have made all the payments.

High-Balling the Value of the Trade-in Allowance

High-balling is a technique used by an automobile salesperson who offers a shopper an extra-high trade-in allowance on his or her present car to create interest in a vehicle even though the offer may later be repudiated by the salesperson's manager. The **high ball** is the high trade-in allowance, a price in excess of the used car's real value. The high offer is made in an effort to keep the potential customer in the showroom seriously interested in purchasing a newer automobile.

This is the way the scheme usually works. The buyer desires a new car with a list price of $14,000 and wants to trade in his or her own vehicle worth only $1500. The salesperson offers the buyer an inflated trade-in value of perhaps $3000 toward the new car, and the buyer expects to pay only $11,000 ($14,000 - $3000). The salesperson writes up the contract, gets the person's signature on it, and goes to find the manager, who must okay all sales. The salesperson soon reappears with the manager close behind, shouting at the salesperson and threatening dismissal. The salesperson apologetically explains that the manager would not okay the contract because the trade-in price was mistakenly misquoted. The buyer then ends up buying the new car at a still high net price, say $12,000 (instead of the $11,000 previously bargained amount), and goes home feeling good about the price he or she paid for the car and glad he or she could help the salesperson out of the predicament with the manager. The result of this high-ball sale is that the dealer gains an extra $500 because the buyer gave up $12,000 in cash plus a trade-in car worth $1,500 for something he or she might have easily bought for $13,000 instead of the $14,000 list price with some honest bargaining.

Low-Balling the Price of a New Vehicle

Low-balling is an unscrupulous technique used by a salesperson who offers to sell a shopper a product, such as an automobile, at an unusually low and unrealistic price that will not be honored when the customer actually wants to make the purchase. The suggestion of a low-price deal is made in an effort to keep the potential customer in the showroom and seriously interested in purchasing an automobile. Again, as with high-balling, the salesperson returns with a contract rejected by the sales manager. Then the price rises, after the customer has had his or her heart set on that particular automobile. Many times the customer still goes ahead and buys at a price somewhat higher than it would be with good bargaining.

> **CONSUMER UPDATE:**
> **Odometer Fraud**
> The U.S. Department of Transportation reports that a high percentage of late-model used cars have odometers that have been turned back. **Odometer fraud** occurs when an odometer is rolled back or disconnected and when incorrect information is given about the accuracy of the odometer reading. The federal Odometer Law requires that the odometer reading be entered on the automobile's title in all states. You should never make a purchase decision solely on the miles shown on the odometer; have a trusted mechanic go over a car prior to purchase.

Automobile Repairs

Auto repairs is one of the top five areas of consumer complaints to government agencies. This occurs in part because most people know little about the operational aspects of an automobile, hence they are especially vulnerable to automobile repair deceptions. For example, when a transmission specialist shows a car owner metal filings that purportedly came from the transmission pan, do you know whether the transmission actually needs replacing? If a service station attendant along the interstate highway points out a leak on a shock absorber, does the car really need new shocks?

A frequent transmission deception has to do with a common method of checking them, known as, "**RCI**," or **remove, check, and install**. Consumers wind up paying $75 to $250 in RCI charges and perhaps another $300 to $1000 for transmission repairs. The misrepresentation occurs when the transmission personnel knows the extent of the needed repairs after road testing a car, checking the transmission pan, and conducting an external check of the transmission system. Yet they do not tell the consumer. Instead, they say they cannot give an estimate for repairs until after they do an RCI procedure, which actually is unnecessary. Other recurring problems in this industry include making unnecessary repairs and charging for work not performed.

Consumers with automobiles that need repairs usually have more success patronizing businesses that have mechanics certified in specialties by the National Institute for Automotive Excellence, which is an independent voluntary certification program for mechanics. Almost all states have automobile repair laws requiring shops to give consumers a written estimate of anticipated charges, to return parts that were replaced, and to obtain advance permission from the consumer before completing work that was not foreseen when the estimate was made. This topic is detailed in Chapter 11.

Chapter 6

Investment Swindles

Many consumers are lured into investments that are bad deals for them but great for the salespersons. There are hundreds of business opportunities and investments that are just wrong for particular investors; others are downright swindles. People are talked into these scams and ripoffs by professional salespersons who are armed to the teeth with dazzling statistics, great promises, and impressive references that seem to confirm the illusions they present. These sellers are masters at manipulation, and they are prepared to provide smooth and seemingly logical answers for every objection raised. The professional swindler always offers reassuring comments to smoothly convince consumers to part with their money. This chapter examines the lures used by investment swindlers and tips on how to avoid financial swindles, as well as a number of specific investment ripoffs and frauds: Ponzi schemes, pyramid schemes, multi-level network marketing investments, chain letters, referral rebate sales, precious metals and oil & gas deals, penny stock schemes, business opportunity schemes, work-at-home schemes, deceptions and biases in financial planning, distant land for sale, and timesharing vacation real estate.

The Investment Swindler's Game

Consumers who invest their money are typically looking to achieve two things: (1) getting as high a return as possible (in interest, dividends and/or a long term appreciation in the value of the investment), and (2) safety. Swindlers attract unsuspecting investors with the promise of an unusually high return.

Investing consumers should be highly skeptical when an investment opportunity emphasizes:

- A very high yield or return
- A quick return
- "Secured principal" is guaranteed
- Approved by the Internal Revenue Service or "IRA approved"
- A "once in a lifetime" opportunity
- Assurances of good locations for vending machines or display racks
- No experience necessary (but send money)
- Promises of an "exclusive territory," or
- The chance to "get in on the ground floor"

Offers for "financial opportunities of a lifetime" are usually exactly that--the consumer's one good chance to lose a lot of money. Most such offers promise high profits for those with little or no business experience. Unfortunately, the investing consumer ends up with the experience, while the promoter earns the high profits.

Among the many scams are those for "investments" in rare coins, art, precious metals, gold and silver contracts, commodities, foreign currencies, off-shore investment funds, "prime" bank notes, oil and gas lease programs, wireless cable television, interactive video and data service television licenses, cellular telephones, specialized mobile radio (SMR), invention promotion, Rembrandt prints, penny stocks, land sales, gum ball machines, pay telephones, electronic games, pop corn vending machines, and display racks for greeting cards or compact discs. Worthless collectibles are popular too, such as 1957 Chevy miniatures, china dolls, and painted dishes. Some schemes are employing holy themes, such as offering divinely inspired investment advice.

A **swindler** is an unscrupulous promoter who concocts an investment scheme that has zero possibility of making money for anyone other than the schemer. Swindlers cheat people out of money or property, and many of them are very good at it. Some swindlers are outright crooks. Others start out to be honest people but wind up sacrificing their ethics for the fast buck of an investment scam. Still others start out with legitimate intentions, but when those go sour because of bad design or poor management, they abscond with the investor's money.

The result of all swindles is the same—the investing consumer loses. Consumers lose because their personal greed exceeds their caution and they believe what they want to believe. The sales techniques used by swindlers are effective; they have to be. Swindlers try to convince consumer-investors of several things: (1) the plan will produce large profits, (2) there is low risk, (3) they are confident you are going to make money, and (4) it is urgent that the consumer act right now. The swindler wants to manipulate the consumer's feelings so he or she feels obligated to go through the deal at an early stage, because those who act before thinking carefully become victims.

Investment swindlers reach their victims in the same ways used by legitimate firms--by telephone, direct mail, referrals, advertisements, on-line investment bulletin boards (reached via America Online, CompuServe and Prodigy), and the appearance of being reputable. Investment swindlers often place classified advertisements in newspapers and magazines or run local television and radio commercials; some run large, expensive advertisements in what one would think would be reputable publications, such as *USA Today*. The ads invite the prospective investor to call an 800 number where they hear the sales pitch.

Shady financial people often get started by establishing their trustworthiness with early investors to obtain referrals to others. Some swindlers even join local civic groups, giving the appearance of legitimacy.

CONSUMER UPDATE:
Watch Out for Telemarketing Recovery Room Scams!

Consumers who have lost money through prize promotions, merchandise sales, investment swindles, and so-called charity drives often have their names put on a "sucker's list" which is sold to other telemarketers so they can be victimized again. These lists contain an amazing amount of detailed information, including name, address, telephone number, the dollars spent on the scam, and sometimes even a credit card number.

This is called a **recovery fee scam** where they falsely promise that, for a fee or a donation to a specified charity, they will recover the consumer's lost investment money, or the product or prize never received. Typically, the telemarketer will call claiming to represent a government agency or consumer organization and report that the thieves have been caught and that their remaining assets have been frozen. The salesperson then says, "For only $250 (or $1000) in attorney's fees (or a charitable donation), we can 'recover' at least one-half of the money you originally lost, and perhaps all of it." Other promoters state that they already are holding the money for you. After the swindler disappears with the recovery fee, the consumer has been scammed a second time. The promoter's telephone pitch should be rephrased to begin, "Congratulations! You have been selected to lose even more money." This unscrupulous practice is also known as "reloading" or "double-scamming". Believe it or not, there also is a re-recovery scam where people pretend to be FBI agents (or U.S. attorneys or IRS agents) who ask for fees to cover "taxes" on their recovered money.

Tips on How to Avoid Financial Swindles

To avoid being taken by investment deceptions, the first line of defense is to ask a lot of questions, and ask them until you get satisfactory answers. Unfortunately, most swindlers are adept at evading questions and giving dishonest answers. They also are good at making themselves difficult to investigate. To check out an investment opportunity, write or telephone the local police, Better Business Bureau, financial editor of your local newspaper, Office of Consumer Affairs, state securities administrator, and such self-regulatory agencies as the National Association of Securities Dealers, National Futures Association, and Securities and Exchange Commission (SEC). The SEC receives over 35,000 complaints about investments each year. If you suspect something in an investment offer is not quite right, report it to the appropriate authorities and regulatory agencies.

Follow these suggestions to avoid getting involved in a bad investment:

- Ignore any deal that sounds too good and hang up the telephone on sales calls;
- Never make an investment based on an unsolicited telephone call;
- If an investment promoter seems to able to predict the future, it is a scam;
- Be wary of hot tips, especially from acquaintances and fellow members of church, fraternal and other organizations;
- Make a close and cautious examination of any investment;
- Demand to see a prospectus or risk-disclosure statement that describes the risks involved in an investment;
- Get oral promises in writing;
- Check out the claims and the person making the claims;
- Verify the history of the firm selling the investment;
- If an investment sounds unfamiliar, get the opinion of a trusted financial advisor;
- Don't invest in anything unless you understand it and can see it;
- Find out who is earning commissions and management fees on the deal, as well as how much they amount to; and
- Monitor the progress of any investment you make.

CONSUMER UPDATE:
Financial Planning Seminars—Ripoffs?

A growing number of schemes have as their sole purpose to sell overpriced business-type manuals at seminars. It takes most victims of investment schemes months to realize that they have been ripped off.

People sometimes pay $10 or $20 to attend a half day or whole day seminar titled, "Low Down Payment Real Estate" or "Invest for Success" or "Improve the Quality of Your Life" held at a local motel. Most meetings are free, although some charge a fee of $10 to $39 (sometimes even $100) to attend. These seminars are often sponsored by those who run infomercials on television or place large and expensive advertisements in local newspapers, which always include testimonials from "satisfied" customers. You may even be sent "complimentary tickets" in the mail. Promoters offer these "free seminars" to entice potential customers to attend. As a sales incentive, consumers are given a "rebate check" that may be used to pay part of the cost of any purchase made during the sales presentation. Once in attendance, you will be met by motivational speakers, upbeat loud music, testimonials from the believers, and some shills who are usually the first ones to "buy and sign on the dotted line". When the seminar is over, the promoters move on to the next town.

The question is usually not whether a seminar is fraudulent, but whether it is a ripoff. After paying out the money-to attend the seminar, for the books, cassettes and videotapes, and perhaps for a membership to receive future counseling or advice-does the purchaser get his or her money's worth? Some will say "Yes," but most, after only a few weeks or months, will reach the conclusion, "Absolutely Not!" Instead, they have paid way too much money for the value received-they've been ripped off.

Chapter 6: Investment Swindles 57

Ponzi Schemes[1]

The Ponzi scheme is named for Charles A. Ponzi, who defrauded hundreds of people in the 1920s by paying off old "investors" with money coming in from new "investors." A **Ponzi scheme** is an investment scam in which the victims are promised an unusually high rate of return in only a few months and are duped into thinking that they will earn this return for a long time period. The earliest investors actually receive good returns, sometimes with their own money, which when paid attract more investors. In reality, there is no investment because the promoter is using the money taken from the many later investors to pay high returns to the few first investors before absconding with the remaining funds. The major factor in the eventual collapse of a Ponzi scheme is that there is no significant source of income other than from new "investors". The Ponzi swindler may operate his or her scheme for some time before disappearing with all the "investments" or revealing the bad news that the investments all went "sour".

The 40,000 investors who put over $32 million in International Loan Network (ILN) during the early 1990s, with promises of returns of 500 percent or more on real estate deals, lost 90 percent of their money before the SEC froze their assets.

Typical Ponzi schemes include so-called investments in industrial wine for use in manufacturing salad dressings, and the buying and selling of race horses, collectible art, and precious metals traded in foreign markets. Consumers are led to invest in Ponzi schemes by promises of 30 to 100 percent profits in perhaps only 6 months. As some early investors take out their profits, others are encouraged to leave their profits in the "investment" to accumulate to even greater sums. When too many investors want to take their profits, the promoter disappears with the money.

CONSUMER UPDATE:
Beware of "Educational Programs" on Insurance and Investments

There is a *Solicitation and Conduct of Personal Commercial Affairs* order that encourages commanders to make qualified personnel and facilities available for counseling military members on loans, consumer credit transactions, and insurance matters. The military aims to encourage thrift, financial responsibility, and sound financial planning.

The services of representatives of credit unions, banks, and approved nonprofit military associations (provided such associations are not underwritten by a commercial insurance company) may be used for military personnel subject to prior approval. Under no circumstances will services of commercial agents, including loan, finance, insurance, or investment companies, be used for these purposes.

Commanding officers are charged with enforcing both the spirit and letter of the law. However, some businesses try to get around this clear instruction by offering "educational" programs on insurance and investments. Beware of the sales pitches that accompany some of these presentations.

*Dean Brassington, Navy Family Services Center, Norfolk, Virginia

---

[1] Helpful information for this and the following two sections came from: *Pyramid Schemes: Not What They Seem!* (Direct Selling Education Foundation), *Tips on Multi-Level Marketing (How to Tell a Legitimate Opportunity From a Pyramid Scheme)* (Better Business Bureau), and *How to Avoid Ponzi and Pyramid Schemes* (U.S. Securities and Exchange Commission).

Pyramid Schemes are Illegal

Pyramid schemes operate on the fallacious assumption that the so-called investors all can make money by selling "distributorships" to others. For example, the promoter offers people the chance to invest by purchasing "distributorships," say at $1000 each. Being a distributor gives the person the exclusive right to sell distributorships to other investors for $1000 each and to sell certain products to the public. Each $1000 received from selling new distributorships is then split on a 50-50 basis with the promoter. Thus, theoretically, each distributor can recoup his or her initial $1000 investment by selling only two distributorships.

Initially, this appears that this can go on forever with all "investors" making money. Pyramid schemes offer the appeal of quick and enormous profits to the participants. But, since the offer must be made to many people, like a seemingly endless chain, the mathematical progression quickly reaches ridiculous numbers. In fact, the number of "investors" that it takes to keep this scheme going quickly exceeds the population of the world. This is shown in the illustration below which assumes that the promoter initially sells distributorships to six persons, each of whom brings in an additional six investors every month.

Lots of "investors" are motivated to participate in pyramid schemes because each new participant pays for the chance to advance to the top to profit from payments of others who might join later. The illustration above also shows why the pyramid scam is so lucrative to the original promoters. Those at the top of the pyramid of "investors" quickly receive a lot of money. The scam works for the promoter because large numbers of people at the bottom of the pyramid pay money to a few people at the top. There is no way the "investors" coming in at the lower levels in a pyramid investment scheme can make any money, and this is why they are illegal. If one joins at level three or four, for example, the odds are almost impossible that an "investor" can ever profit. Since it is mathematically impossible for this "investment" to succeed, it is classically fraudulent.

Month	Participants
1	6
2	36
3	216
4	1,296
5	7,776
6	46,656
7	279,936
8	1,679,616
9	10,077,696
10	60,466,176
11	362,797,056 (far exceeds U.S. population)
12	2,179,782,336
13	13,060,694,016 (more than double the world population)

No matter how it is described, this pyramid stuff always collapses! Plus, victims of pyramid schemes usually do not know where they are in the pyramid or that the odds are heavily stacked against them.

Chapter 6: Investment Swindles 59

> **CONSUMER UPDATE:**
> **The Airplane Pyramid Scheme**
> One pyramid scheme that has been seen in many communities is "Airplane"; it is also called "Friends Helping Friends". Here the promotor explains that there is one pilot, two co-pilots, four crew members, and eight passengers, where the pilot captain is at the apex of a four-tier pyramid. Newcomers pay perhaps a $1000 fee to buy one of the eight passenger seats, shown as empty squares on a diagram. In theory, each pilot collects $8000-eight times his or her original "investment". Every person in the pyramid is responsible for recruiting more people to join the airplane. After all eight passenger spaces have been sold, the pilot leaves the airplane with his or her illegal profits. The two co-pilots then can split the original airplane investment game in half and move up to pilot status, thus creating two airplane games and beginning the process anew. Once again, at the bottom are new passenger seats to be sold at $1000 each. In theory, each of the passengers will eventually move up to a pilot captain's position so they can collect the big money. With this pyramid scheme, it is hard to tell the scammers from the scammees as they constantly change with new people joining and leaving the airplane.

Telltale signs of pyramid investment schemes is that (1) they rely upon new investors to pay returns, commissions, or bonuses, (2) there is a need for an inexhaustible supply of new investors, and (3) there is a conspicuous absence of a product or substantial efforts to make profits through productive work, the sale of the products. The most common pyramid schemes are investments, chain letters, and referral sales, and these are discussed below.

Some pyramid investment schemes are made to look like multi-level marketing businesses. **Multi-level network marketing** is a legitimate sales method that uses a network of independent distributors to sell consumer products and the bulk of income is earned from product sales. In an attempt to avoid prosecution by government agencies, pyramid schemes try to look legitimate. Therefore, many pyramid investment schemes do have a line of products to sell while the promoter claims to be in the business of selling the products to consumers. The products often are things like cosmetics, hair care, vitamins, miracle products, and exotic cures.

The key difference between a multi-level network marketing investment and a pyramid scheme is the illegal investment schemes make their money primarily from the proceeds of new "investors". These are the new recruits to the so-called business. The real motivation in a pyramid investment scheme is to recruit new investors, not to sell products.[2]

Multi-Level Network Marketing Investments are Legitimate

Multi-level network marketing is a legitimate sales method that uses a network of independent distributors to sell consumer products. Sales are usually made in customers'

---

[2]The largest "private investment fund" in Russia, known as MMM, collapsed recently as the value of the fund was lowered from $56 to 46 cents. (That is greater than a 100 to 1 drop in value.) This left between 1 and 10 million investors defrauded by what was a pyramid scheme. MMM advertised on Russian television even after repeated government warnings that MMM was a scam.

homes. These are bona fide business opportunities, such as Mary Kay Cosmetics, Amway, Shaklee, and Herbalife.[3]

As a distributor, the investor in a multi-level marketing opportunity is an independent business person, setting working hours, and earning money selling products or services supplied by an established company. In a multi-level business, distributors also have the opportunity to develop and manage their own sales forces by recruiting, training, and supplying others to sell. A distributor's compensation then is based upon fees earned for recruiting others into the business, commissions earned on personal sales, and a percentage of the sales of the recruited sales force. To be legitimate, a multi-level marketing investor must earn the bulk his or her profits from product sales.

Here is an example of how a multi-level marketing opportunity works. An investor puts up $2000 to buy into and become a dealer of a product line, perhaps some cosmetics or household cleaning items. By going door-to-door, the person investing in this business can sell some products that the public might like and make a little money. The investor is further told that if he or she recruits other persons to invest $2000 each to start up a distributorship, the first investor will receive a $500 bonus for each recruit and a 5- to 10-percent commission on the wholesale value of all the sales of the newer investor-distributors.

Key differences between illegal pyramid schemes and multi-level marketing opportunities are: (1) the bulk of the income in a multi-level marketing business comes from product sales, (2) legitimate companies sell quality products and do repeat business with their customers, (3) start-up fees for legitimate businesses are small, (4) legitimate companies that require inventory purchases will usually repurchase any unsold items, and (5) legitimate companies want to make money with the investor and expand the overall market for the business.

Chain Letters are Pyramid Schemes

Chain letters involve the sending of money through the mail with the chance that nothing will be received in turn. These are illegal and they operate on the same fallacious principle as pyramid schemes. As a result, the great majority of participants must lose. Typically, a letter from some distant city arrives addressed to you with instructions to send a sum of money (perhaps $2 or $20) to the top name on an enclosed list of perhaps five names. Then you are to eliminate that name, add your own name and address at the bottom of the list, and mail copies of the new list to all the people on it. The appeal is that your name will be added to a multitude of subsequent lists by other people in the chain and you will receive enormous sums of money within a month or so.

Another chain letter scam says, "Earn $19,500 by buying a $5 computer program called Network!, copy it onto floppy disks, and send it on to five people." The letter also says that the five people who receive the copied disk will in turn make five more copies and send them on, and so on, until thousands of people have the program. You will make money because those thousands will send $5 each to the originator of the chain letter. Selling a product, such as a computer disk, is a gimmick to try to avoid the appearance of an illegal pyramid scheme.

---

[3]The 100,000 sales force of NuSkin distributors have been accused by the attorney general of Michigan of being an illegal pyramid franchise.

The reality of the mathematical progression of numbers tells us that the only people getting rich off this venture are its earliest promoters. Typically, the narrative also falsely claims that, "This is a perfectly legal enterprise!" or "Approved by the Postal Service!" Anyone who participates is not only out the $2, $5, or whatever amount (plus the cost of stamps), but his or her name and address is now clearly recorded, which makes it easier for a government fraud unit to locate should they investigate this particular scam. Chain letters are a violation of the mail fraud statute-up to five years in prison and fines of up to $1000, or both. The government generally goes after the chain letter organizers, not the participants who are the victims.

Referral Rebate Sales are Pyramid Schemes

Referral rebate sales are a variation of the illegal pyramid scheme, and it occurs when a buyer is induced to sign a contract with the promise that he or she will receive a rebate or other consideration for each additional customer referred to the seller who later makes a similar purchase. Payment of the consideration is contingent upon a subsequent sale. For example, a buyer might sign a contract to purchase a $1000 stereo system with the promise that $50 will be credited to the $1000 debt for every person that the buyer refers to the seller who purchases the stereo system.

The impossible mathematics of the pyramid scheme is again seen with this variation-referral rebate sales-and that is why they are illegal. Usually exempt from these laws are referrals for real estate, automobile and insurance sales, areas where it is traditional for sellers to pay their customers finder's fees for referrals.

Precious Metals and Oil & Gas Deals

Consumers are typically persuaded by telemarketing sales specialists to invest in gold, silver, or platinum with promises of enormous returns because the caller predicts that the market price is about to skyrocket during the next few days or weeks. The salesperson may offer to let you pay a portion of the cost of the metal in cash, perhaps 20 percent, and arrange a loan for the remainder. While oil and gas leases are legitimate business opportunities, what the telemarketers are promoting is often a scam. More often than not the "investment opportunity" is to pay for drilling equipment set on worthless land where there are no known petroleum deposits. Wise consumers never invest by telephone.

Penny Stock Schemes

Penny stock swindles cost American investors an estimated $2 billion a year, according to a nationwide study by state securities regulators. **Penny stock schemes** involve the sale of cheaply priced stock, typically under $5 a share and sometimes less than $1, in thinly traded small corporations (sometimes the companies are nonexistent, financially distressed, or even bankrupt) by unscrupulous brokers who use high-pressure telemarketing tactics to persuade novice investors to buy shares at huge markups. Later, the sellers pump up buyer demand for the stock which has relatively few shares available for trading. This abrupt surge in demand artificially inflates the price of the shares of

> **CONSUMER UPDATE:**
> **Information Highway Scams**
> Chain letters, penny stock swindles, unregistered stocks, phony oil leases, fantasy ostrich farms, pyramid schemes, and other get-rich stratagems are on the global computer electronic mail networks, such as Internet, computer bulletin boards, and on-line services. Prodigy's Money Talk bulletin board, CompuServe, and America Online do not screen messages for fraud. Con artists have adapted yesterday's old scams to today's technology. Federal and state government "cybercops" are stopping scams every month, but more and more are popping up. Complaints to the North American Securities Administrators Association, an organization of state regulators, (202-737-0900), will be directed to the correct agency.

stock. The schemer then dump their shares at the peak price, leaving their victims with worthless or nearly worthless stock.

These inexpensive securities are sold in the over-the-counter market because they are not listed or traded on a stock exchange or quoted on the National Association of Securities Dealers Automated Quotation (NASDAQ) system. Penny stocks are traded in the over-the-counter market where volume and price information is generally not easily collected or made available to the public. Brokerage firms trading penny stocks can usually provide information only about trades they make. Published *pink sheets*, a daily listing, contain pricing information on 13,000 penny stocks, but the information does not necessarily indicate the price for which you can sell your stock.

Many penny stocks are sold by telemarketers making unsolicited telephone calls and using high-pressure sales techniques. Sometimes unregistered stockbrokers set up shop in garages or motels, telling consumers that they have inside information and that this unique opportunity is available only for a short time period. With only a single brokerage firm or just a few firms involved, they find it easy to buy and sell in such a way to manipulate stock prices, creating artificial markets and marking up stock prices by 100 percent or more. Sometimes the penny stocks being promoted exist only on paper. Penny stock brokerage firms earn their profits by charging markups above the price the firm is paying for the stock. Undisclosed, excessive markups are illegal but common. Some penny stock schemes have links to organized crime.

A rule of the Securities and Exchange Commission (SEC) states that penny stock orders solicited by a broker cannot be completed until the customer sends back a written approval for each of his or her first three purchases. Several things must be done before a broker executes a transaction. Brokers are required to verify a customer's financial situation and investment experience and maintain those records. They must give investors a written document spelling out consumer rights and remedies should the investment go awry. The document also should disclose what the broker will earn.

Penny stock brokers usually will strongly resist your desire to sell your stocks for cash. You may be unable to reach the salesperson when you want to sell, or your salesperson may refuse to sell your stock unless you agree to buy another penny stock.

In most states, penny stocks can be offered for sale without being registered with an appropriate government securities agency. The SEC estimates that one in three penny stock brokerage firms commits serious abuses against their investors.

A New York judge recently barred Power Securities Corporation, a national penny stock brokerage house, from soliciting new business in that state after Attorney General

Robert Abrams presented evidence that the company defrauded millions of dollars from thousands of investors. Abrams said that, "Deception and fraudulent conduct are at the very heart of their business." Former penny-stock king Meyer Blinder recently was sentenced to 46 months in jail on racketeering and fraud charges. Last year Robert E. Brennan, who ran First Jersey Securities, and was pursued for 16 years by securities regulators, was finally put out of business and ordered to pay $71 million in fines for defrauding 500,000 clients with his 1200 person sales force. In television ads Brennan used to jump out of the pilot's seat of a helicopter to invite investors to "come grow with us."

Business Opportunity Schemes

Swindlers who promote business opportunities-often distributorships-obtain large sums of money from their victims. The promoter emphasizes how quickly you can start earning a large income, especially since there is so little competition for the product. The way the scam works is to sell the investor the equipment, product, or program, which is often overpriced and inappropriate for the marketplace, and then ignore pleas for assistance by the investor because the promoter is only interested in the initial sale.

Many fraudulent business opportunity schemes are promoted as franchises. A **franchise** is a right officially granted by a manufacturer or dealer to an investor to sell his products, and often there are territorial limits within which the privilege may be exercised. The signing of many legal documents between the investor and the promoter gives an added allure of credibility, whether warranted or not.

For example, a promoter may offer an investor an exclusive territory for placing vending machines, video bowling games, or display racks for greeting cards in exclusive locations. All the investor has to do is to replenish the goods, keep the machines clean, and collect the money. The reality is that the products do not sell well and the machines (typically old equipment) frequently break down. The swindlers even give fake references so that potential investors can telephone them. Convinced investors quickly become victims.

Work-at-Home Scams

Swindlers practice their pathetic motives on people who least need to be ripped off, those unable to work away from their homes because of difficulties in obtaining transportation, or because of health or family responsibilities. Advertisements for work-at-home schemes often appear in the classified sections of newspapers and magazines as well as on matchbook covers. Such "Earn Money at Home" opportunities sound lucrative and easy to do in the privacy of one's home. They promise to purchase the completed items. They promise good incomes, too, but they lie.

Popular work-at-home scams include stuffing envelopes, clipping grocery coupons, putting gift items together, sewing neckties, raising chinchillas (to sell the fur pelts), gilding greeting cards, and home assembly of crafts. Products completed by people working at home are later refused by the promoter because, "They do not meet our quality standards," and the worker is left with lots of worthless items. The purpose of the promoter is to profit by selling the overpriced materials or equipment needed, selling instructions on how to perform the at-home tasks, and (believe it or not!) selling instructions on how to buy classified advertisements to run the same work-at-home scheme.

Deceptions and Biases in Financial Planning

Fraud and abuse exists in the financial planning industry according to the North American Securities Administrators Association. The organization reported that 79 state enforcement actions revealed that 22,000 consumers, mostly middle-income people, lost almost $400 million over a two-year time period. Problem areas included financial planners who were unqualified, those who were moonlighting from another job and knew little about the field, those with a history of legal problems, those who were driven to sell commission-based products instead of providing more objective advice, and Ponzi schemers.

Although many financial planners have professional credentials, perhaps as an attorney, a certified public accountant, an insurance broker, or a registered investment advisor, there is no license to become a financial planner. Anyone can use the term, even convicted felons. Most financial planners do not have to pass any examinations or meet any educational or experience standards. The "bad apples" in the financial planning industry are making life harder for the legitimate operators, as well as for the investing public.

The Consumer Federation of America (CFA) is calling for Congress to act "to protect consumers from fraudulent, self-dealing, and incompetent financial planners" by strengthening existing regulatory structures. CFA estimates that at least $500 million was lost to fraudulent brokers in a recent year, and "at least that much was misinvested because of incompetent or self-interested advice." CFA's Barbara Roper says that, "If the consumer is to be protected, a better job must be done up front to detect and deter such abuses."

Almost all investments and some types of life insurance throw off sizable commissions. The prospect of a big commission has motivated many a salesperson into promoting the wrong investment products. Of course, there are many financial planners, including those who earn commissions, who are well qualified to give investors excellent advice. Investors always should investigate anyone in whom they are placing their trust for investment advice.

Your most objective advice in the financial planning industry can be obtained from a **fee-only financial planner**. This is a person who earns no commissions and works solely on a fee-for-service basis, charging a specified fee for the services provided. All other financial planners earn their income, wholly or in part, from the commissions on investment products "sold" to investors. The national association of fee-only financial planners is the National Association of Personal Financial Advisors (1130 Lake Cook Road, Suite 150, Buffalo Grove, IL 60089; telephone 800-366-2732).

Distant Land for Sale

Nearly worthless land is often sold, sight unseen, to gullible investors in distant states. Sellers set up shop in a motel and entice people to come hear their presentation, usually by offering free meals and prizes. After showing a short film or slides about the beautiful property in Florida, Texas, Colorado, Vermont, Oregon, or some other distant

> **CONSUMER UPDATE:**
> **Financial-Advice Radio and Television Talk Shows**
> A number of financial-advice radio and television talk shows are nothing more than cleverly disguised commercials for the businesses of the hosts and the so-called guest experts. Some are infomercials. Hosts buy air time and give the impression of offering impartial advice. The well-respected NBC talk-show host Bruce Williams and Business Radio Network's Don McDonald do not peddle specific investments and they identify commercials as commercials. Some talk-show hosts are nothing more than salespersons.

place, the promoters deceptively state: "This is terrific investment property even if you never build on it yourself" and "Previously sold lots have doubled in value in only 36 months." Then they try to get potential buyers to sign on the dotted line for purchase contracts.

One important aspect in many deceptions is the use of shills. A **shill** is a person who works as a decoy in a confidence game by posing as a customer or an innocent bystander. During land sales presentations, as well as during many other types of deceptions where a group of potential victims is present, one or two shills will stand up and say, "Yes, I want to get in on this deal. Where do I sign up?" Sometimes there are more shills in the audience than victims, and when the unknowing victim turns to the person sitting at the next table and asks for advice on what to do, the shill willingly gives advice. Many states have cooling-off period laws during which consumers can change their minds about buying.

Timesharing Vacation Real Estate

Timesharing is promoted as investment property; however, most of the time it turns out to be a ripoff for the investor because profits for consumers in this industry exist only rarely. **Timesharing** is the use of a vacation home for a limited, preplanned time. About 14 million consumers own timeshares. For $5000 to $20,000 buyers can purchase one week's use of luxury vacation housing furnished right down to the salt and pepper shakers. Vacationers also pay an annual maintenance fee for each week of ownership, perhaps $400 or $500 a year. Many people buy, falsely thinking that they are making a real estate purchase that will appreciate in value when what they are really making is a decision on where to spend future vacations.

A serious problem arises in **non-deeded timesharing**. This is a right-to-use purchase agreement entered into between the seller and the consumer that permits a limited, preplanned timesharing period of use that is actually only a vacation lease, license, or club membership, which only last a certain number of years. It does not grant legal real estate ownership interests to the purchaser, but instead provides a long-term lease of a hotel, suite, condominium, or other accommodation. When the lease runs out, often in 20 to 25 years, the non-deeded timesharing consumer has no legal claim to anything. The bad news begins earlier if the real owner of the property (the developer) goes bankrupt, because the purchasers (the lessees) have a zero ownership claim to the property. The consumers have no more legal rights than other unsecured creditors, and in all likelihood, they lose previous payments and their leases on their vacation properties. Timeshare purchasers should only buy **deeded timesharing** units because the buyer actually owns part of the property.

So-called **real estate liquidators** are scam artists that take advantage of people with hard-to-sell properties, such as undeveloped land and timeshares. The promise is to connect the owner with prospective buyers. Some operators tell owners that their nationwide computer network contains the names of several buyers who are interested in their properties. Other promoters promise to sell the timeshare during the following twelve months for a price equal to or greater than the amount originally paid. They sometimes promise to give the property owner a $1000 savings bond certificate if they fail to sell the property (and from reading this book, you know the savings bond is worthless). After collecting a $250 to $1000 **advance fee**, the promoters simply do not refund the money, even though property owners were "guaranteed a 100% refund" if a sale did not occur.

Resale of timeshare properties generally sell for about 50 to 70 percent of what the owner paid, according to the head of a trade association trying to clean up the industry's image. A reputable and large broker of timeshares, Vacation Concepts, reports that it sells only 10 to 15 percent of its listings. A large Florida seller of timeshares, Independent Timeshare Sales, reports that its commissions are 20 to 25 percent.

Some consumers buy timeshares because they believe that they can easily and inexpensively trade use of their properties for use of other properties in more exotic places. The largest timeshare exchange business is Resort Condominiums. It charges a $200 initiation fee, a $59-a-year membership fee, and another $84 for each week of an exchange. Consumers sometimes wind up paying substantial fees to advertise and trade use of their properties.

Florida has a law that puts time-share resale agents under the direct authority of a state regulatory agency. Licensed agents have to spell out in writing all services, conditions, and fees and are prohibited from offering guarantees to sell time-shares by a specific time or at a set price. Many states now have cooling-off period laws, often 3 to 5 days, during which consumers can change their minds about investing in timeshares. Such legal protections for investing consumers, however, are not available in all states.

Chapter 7

Legal and Moral Rights of Consumers

Consumer rights are important because they empower consumers to protect themselves in the marketplace. A **right** is an entitlement to something or to be treated in some particular way. Even though Americans have a number of consumer rights, we have a tendency to be unaware of them and then to not exercise them.

If consumers want to function effectively in the American marketplace—especially to get their money's worth—they must know their rights and exercise their responsibilities, and, when necessary, they must seek redress when any of their rights are violated. For example, a lack of understanding about how warranties operate can leave consumers at a distinct disadvantage. Alternatively, an empowered consumer can be a powerful regulator of the economic marketplace. Consumers have a great number of legal rights that are provided under statutory and common law.

Legal Rights of Consumers

Consumers have three types of legal rights: (1) **Implied warranties** which arise from common law or by operation of law and need not be specified by the parties,[1] (2) **Express warranties** which arise from contracts (and largely governed in the states by the Uniform Commercial Code and by the federal Magnuson-Moss Warranty Act), and (3) dozens of **statutory rights** which are those provided in written laws and regulations. These are discussed below.

Implied Warranty Rights are Powerful Legal Rights

A **warranty** or **(guarantee)** is a written or oral assurance by the seller of property that the goods or property is of the quality represented or will be as promised. A person who purchases a new clothes dryer, a bicycle, or a stereo system that does not work properly has the legal right to get the problem corrected. If it is not fixed, the consumer has the legal right to get the product fixed, replaced or obtain a refund of money paid. When no remedy occurs, the consumer has a right to bring legal action against the seller.

All states have similar warranty laws mandating an implied warranty *every* time goods are sold by merchants to consumers. Thus, the law requires that merchants provide implied warranties when they sell clothing or bicycles or whatever, but a neighbor selling similar goods at a garage sale does not have to provide such warranties. An **implied warranty** is a written or unwritten promise that the manufacturer implicitly asserts that the product is usable and will not fail during normal use. There are two types.

Warranty of Merchantability

The first type of implied warranty is a **warranty of merchantability**, which means that the consumer has a right to expect that the product is reasonably fit for the ordinary purposes for which the goods are expected to be used. This means that the goods should be in proper condition for sale and that they will perform as they were intended to. For example, a vacuum cleaner is expected to function properly and clean dirt from carpets and rugs. It should vacuum, not just sweep, as with electric brooms. Note that in a number of states, courts have ruled that home builders are responsible for any defects in their work, even if there is no written contract or warranty that makes responsibilities clear. Authority for such a ruling comes under the concept of implied warranty of merchantability, and this legal right can be upheld even *after* a written warranty has expired. In 1990, the U.S. Supreme Court ruled that manufacturers could not unreasonably and unconscionably put short time limits on warranties. Thus, if a consumer believes a new product should have a warranty longer than its written warranty, it probably does.

---

[1] **Common law** is a system of laws originated and developed in England based on court decisions, on the doctrines implicit in those judgments, and on customs and usages rather than on codified written laws.

Warranty of Fitness for a Particular Purpose

The second type of implied warranty is **warranty of fitness for a particular purpose**. Here the seller is presumed to know the particular purpose for which a buyer is purchasing the goods *and* knows that the buyer has relied upon the seller's knowledge, skill, and judgment to select and sell appropriate goods. In order for a warranty of fitness for a particular purpose to be created between the seller and the buyer, the seller should have "reason to know" the buyer's purpose for purchasing the product and the buyer must rely on the seller's skill or judgment in selecting the goods.

This important legal right of warranty of fitness for a particular purpose protects consumers who go to buy a product or service from a merchant and trust the advice they receive, buy it, and then suffer because it does not perform as anticipated. For example, Jean Johnson, from Logan, Utah, goes to an electronics store to buy a television antenna and tells the salesperson that she wants to pick up the Salt Lake City stations. After installing it on the roof, she finds that the television works, but the pictures coming from the Salt Lake stations are just not clear. This is a simple case of breach of implied warranty. The store created the contract when Jean relied on the advice of the salesperson, and it is violated because she cannot receive the television picture desired. The store owes her a refund, even if the product has scratches from putting the mast up on the roof.[2]

The same legal rights apply to all types of services. For example, if one is charged $8 for dry cleaning services, it is understood that the soiled clothes should be returned clean. The proprietor has a legal obligation to stand by the quality of the work. If the clothing is not cleaned properly, either they should be processed again or the cost should be refunded. To avoid the warranty of fitness for a particular purpose, some dry cleaners are careful to tell customers that they do not remove "stubborn stains".

Express Warranty Rights are Enforceable

In the area of warranties, express warranties are covered by both statutory and common law. An **express warranty** can be created by written or verbal words or by demonstration as it sets out the specific assurances by the manufacturer or seller.[3] Once created, an express warranty is extremely difficult to destroy. **Written express warranties** are statements that specify the name and address of the warrantor, the product or parts covered, the duration of the warranty, and specifically what the warrantor will do, and who will pay for it. Each state has provisions under the Uniform Commercial Code that regulate implied and express warranty rights.

There is a federal statute in the area of warranties also. Sellers who offer warranties on consumer products that cost $15 or more are required to comply with various standards under the Magnuson-Moss Warranty Act. Basically, the federal law demands that a warranty should mean what it says and that the details should be spelled out in

---

[2]McDonald's became the first chain to correctly extend the concept of implied warranties by establishing a formal policy of guaranteeing a free meal for dissatisfied consumers: "If you are not satisfied, we will make it right—or your next meal is on us."

[3]Alperin, H. J. & Chase, R. F. (1986) observe on page 312 in *Consumer Law: Sales Practice and Credit Regulation* (West) that, "a seller creates an express warranty under the Code when he (1) makes any affirmation of fact or promise about the goods, (2) describes the goods, (3) uses a sample of the goods, or (4) uses a model of the goods."

easy-to-understand language. The law requires that guarantees be conspicuously designated as either **full** or **limited**, which immediately gives consumers an indication of the degree of warranty coverage provided. The law also encourages the use of an informal dispute procedure whenever warranty problems arise between sellers and buyers. Consumers who successfully file state or federal lawsuits against warrantors may be awarded their purchase costs, attorney fees, and damages. (Detailed information on consumer rights and remedies under the provisions of the Magnuson-Moss Warranty Act are included in Chapter 12.) As a defense against a warranty claim, a seller may argue that the buyer was given an opportunity for reasonable inspection that was disclaimed by the buyer's inaction.

Those who offer warranties sometimes try to disclaim or repudiate them to make them void. For example, state laws permit a warranty of merchantability to be disclaimed legally if it is done in clear, conspicuous, and specific language. A popular example is when a used automobile is sold **as is**, or with all its faults.

CONSUMER UPDATE:
Unconscionability May Get One Out of a Contract Because the Seller Took Unfair Advantage of the Consumer

Unconscionability is a legal doctrine having to do with unscrupulousness under which the court may invalidate an agreement, or a portion of it, if it is so one-sided as to be unreasonable. Perhaps the seller took advantage of the consumer's ignorance, inability to read, inability to read English, physical infirmity or some recent personal crisis (i.e., death in the family, accident). Unconscionability implies that the consumer believed that he/she had no choice in the buying situation which resulted in the purchasing terms being so one-sided that they unreasonably favored the seller. Examples of unconscionability might include inflated prices, unfair contractual terms, horribly high interest charges and some rent-to-own contracts.

If the bargaining positions of the seller and the buyer were so unequal that the seller took advantage of the consumer, it might be possible to get out of the contract. If the consumer believes a contract to be unconscionable, the following steps are recommended: (1) notify the seller in writing that the deal was unconscionable, (2) do not make any payments, and (3) return the purchased goods and/or tell service providers that such services are no longer needed. The consumer may be sued, but unconscionability may be an excellent defense.

Lots of Other Legal Rights Also Exist

Dozens of federal, state, and local laws, regulations, and ordinances are available to protect consumers, and many of them will be described in the chapters that follow. Listed below are two key legal rights provided for in illustrative statutory laws, and details are provided in Chapters 9 through 14: (1) Consumers have the legal right to find out the reason why they are turned down for credit based on information provided by a credit-reporting agency under provisions of the Fair Credit Reporting Act, and (2) Consumers have the right when unsatisfied with what a manufacturer does about a product warranty complaint to use an informal dispute procedure, as provided for in the Magnuson-Moss Warranty Act.

Chapter 7: *Legal and Moral Rights of Consumers* **71**

**CONSUMER UPDATE:
Rule #1 of Consumer Life—When in Doubt About a Purchase,
Put It On Your Credit Card**

Consumers have the legal right not to pay for a cost of disputed purchase made on a credit card when they complain about it to the merchant and the creditor. This right is provided in the Fair Credit Billing Act. Let your credit card company—VISA, MasterCard, American Express, Discover, whatever—help you fight the merchant or unscrupulous scam operator that provided you with an unsatisfactory purchase that you charged on your credit card. Those credit card users who dispute charges have an excellent chance of getting their money back; those who paid with cash or a check may never again see their money. See Chapter 10 for details.

Moral Rights of Consumers are Legitimate Expectations

In addition to legal rights, consumers have moral rights in the marketplace. **Moral rights** are expectations of consumers that the marketplace will be guided by principles, rules, and standards of good conduct that arise from conscience or a sense of right and wrong. Moral rights are not provided automatically in the marketplace, but they are expected.

General Moral Rights

Some general moral rights include:

- Being treated equitably in the marketplace

- Being treated courteously by salespersons when shopping even though a purchase may not be made

- Being given an opportunity to compare prices and products inside stores without interference

- Being able to buy goods and services with socially acceptable minimum standards of quality

- Being sold products that are safe, both to the consumer and the environment

- Being assured of honesty from merchants in every transaction

- Being assured of a certain degree of privacy

- Being given fair treatment by sellers regardless of economic, political, religious, racial, ethnicity, gender, or youthful appearance

President Kennedy's Consumer Bill of Rights

President John F. Kennedy took the idea of moral rights for consumers a major step forward when he formally proclaimed a "Consumer Bill of Rights" in a speech before the Congress of the United States. The rights as President Kennedy set them down in 1962 are:

The right to choose

The right to safety

The right to be informed

The right to be heard

All subsequent presidents have confirmed to the nation that consumer rights in America are here to stay.

A List of Consumer Rights for All Americans

The moral concerns of Americans about consumer expectations in marketplace transactions have evolved into today's list of eight important consumer rights:

1. **The right to choice**, by which consumers have the right to make an intelligent choice among products and services. This gives consumers the freedom to decide what to buy and how to use it because competitive markets exist that make available a variety of products and services at competitive prices. In those instances where competition is not workable, government regulation should be substituted with the assurance of satisfactory quality and fair prices.

2. **The right to information**, by which consumers have the right to accurate information on which to make a free choice, thus they are provided access to the facts with which to make informed choices while also being protected against fraudulent, deceptive, and misleading information, advertising, labeling, and related practices.

3. **The right to safety**, by which consumers have the right to expect the health and safety of the buyer will be taken into account by those seeking patronage. Thus consumers should be able to assume that products will perform as intended without being hazardous to health or life.

4. **The right to voice**, by which the interests of consumers will be given full and fair consideration in government policy-making situations and expeditious treatment in its administrative tribunals.

5. **The right to redress or remedy**, by which consumers are provided with easily accessible, understandable, and low-cost mechanisms through which grievances and dissatisfactions can be addressed.

6. **The right to environmental health**, by which consumers may consume in an environmentally sound manner and be protected from the ill effects of pollution of the air, earth and water that may occur in the performance of everyday marketplace transactions.

7. **The right to service**, by which consumers may expect convenience, courtesy, and responsiveness to consumer problems and needs and all steps necessary to ensure that products and services meet the quality and performance levels claimed for them.

8. **The right to consumer education**, by which consumers are provided the right to consumer education, without which consumers cannot gain the full benefit of the other consumer rights, which will help all consumers to maximize their resources, become more effective in the marketplace, and to achieve the greatest personal satisfaction.

Chapter 8

How to Resolve Consumer Problems

It is impossible for consumers to go through life without experiencing some difficulties in marketplace transactions. Research shows that approximately one out of four purchases results in some type of problem. People complain for lots of reasons: faulty products, unsafe products, poor product performance, problems with delivery, being shortchanged at the cash register, errors in credit billing statements, communication failures with sellers, ripoffs, misrepresentations, and frauds. Occasionally, consumers just change their minds and want to return products. Consumer affairs offices in business and government are receiving more than twice the number of complaints than they did ten years ago.

Why People Don't Complain

Even though sellers are generally receptive to complaints, many consumers do not complain. People do not complain because they think complaining will not be worth their time, because they think that complaining will not do any good, and because they do not know how or where to complain. Many consumers do not complain because they believe the benefits of complaining will not exceed the costs.

John Goodman, president of Technical Assistance Research Programs (TARP), has research data on customer dissatisfaction. It shows that about one-third of consumer dissatisfaction with a product or service stems from either unfulfilled expectations or lack of knowledge regarding use, another one-third stems from company policies and procedures, and a final one third results from product defects.

The percentage of customers experiencing problems with selected products and services who do not complain are 60 percent for high-priced durable goods, 50 percent for medium-priced durable goods, 37 percent for high priced services, and 45 percent for low-priced services. TARP data further reveal that the average business does not hear from 96 percent of its unhappy customers. For every complaint received at company headquarters, the average business has another 26 customers with problems, at least 6 of which are serious concerns. Depending on the industry, between 65 and 90 percent of non-complainers do not buy from particular businesses again and they never tell the business why. In sum, every complaint represents dozens of dissatisfied customers.

For small consumer problems that resulted in a loss of a few dollars or a minor inconvenience, only 3 percent of consumers complain, 30 percent return the product, and nearly 70 percent either do nothing or discard the product. Research from the A. C. Nielsen Company shows that of those people who experience major consumer problems, such as a financial loss of about $150 or more, about one-third never complain.

Many businesses view consumer complaints as a public relations necessity and fail to use complaints to seriously evaluate the effectiveness of the efforts of the organization. Yet the data provided by consumers who complain offer businesses the unique opportunity to assess the efficiency of their operations and the quality of their products.

Enlightened business leaders view customer complaints as opportunities in disguise. They invite customer complaints and use complaint data in worthwhile ways, because they see that what consumers think about a company is almost more important than the complaint problems themselves. Depending upon the business, it probably takes 5 to 10 times the cost of properly handling a complaint for a company to go out and find a single new customer. Smart business people know that if they are totally consumer-focused and deliver what customers want, everything else falls into place, i.e., sales, profits, bonuses, happy employees. From the business perspective, **consumer satisfaction** is when a customer's needs, wants, and expectations are met or exceeded, and that satisfaction results in repurchases and loyalty to the seller.

Remedies to Resolve Consumer Problems

While laws exist to protect consumers from frauds and misrepresentations, no laws require merchants to offer refunds, exchanges, or credits on merchandise they sell. Before making purchases, shoppers should inquire about the seller's **return policy**. This is the guiding principle or set of procedures used by sellers that explicitly states the conditions under which products can be returned, exchanged, or credited. Policies are often written on sales receipts and posted inside store premises near the cash register; many states have laws requiring the posting of return policies. Most sellers require that products be returned within a limited time period, in good condition, in the original packaging, with a sales receipt; others are more flexible in their conditions. Some companies may require a restocking charge of up to 15 percent of the price and/or prior authorization before you can return an item.

If you buy goods or services that are unsatisfactory and not at the level you expected, ask the seller to take back the goods, if possible, and obtain a refund. If not, ask the seller to reduce the price to accommodate your dissatisfaction. You may ask a seller for a refund or price reduction even if you simply changed your mind. Perhaps you don't like the color after all, or it really doesn't fit the decor of the home, or you spent too much money and need the cash for something else.

Sellers are willing to handle the numerous types of consumer complaints for several reasons: (1) to fulfill the desire to act fairly and honestly in marketplace transactions and maintain a positive reputation, (2) to obtain early warning signals about defects and possible violations of laws, (3) to learn about problems with products or services, so they can be corrected quickly, (4) to avoid bad publicity, particularly from assertive consumers who write letters to third parties (such as government agencies), (5) to reduce third-party liability claims, (6) to keep customers satisfied and loyal (so they will not go to the competition), (7) to increase profits over the long run by making sales to new customers who receive positive word-of-mouth comments from existing customers, and (8) to avoid government regulation and improve relationships with regulators.

Most sellers now realize that doing the job right the first time and effectively handling complaints results in increased consumer satisfaction because these efforts encourage old customers to continue to buy. That kind of reputation also helps bring in new customers.

How to Complain Effectively

Follow these procedures to complain effectively: (1) Pursue your complaint as soon as possible after experiencing dissatisfaction, while events are still fresh in your mind; (2) clearly identify the problem and document it with evidence; (3) if possible, register your complaint with the person responsible for the transaction, otherwise go to that person's boss; (4) explain how you want your complaint resolved (apology, repair, refund, etc.); (5) be courteous and show respect, but be firm and persistent (realizing too that even though you were wronged, there are two sides to every story); (6) be willing to compromise, especially if you will not otherwise benefit; and, (7) be prepared to wait a reasonable amount of time for the responsible person to make a decision on your complaint.

The Complaining Process Should Follow a Sequence

The only way to remedy seller wrongs is for consumers to personally take actions to resolve such matters. Simply put, consumers must complain, and if complaining does not work, they should tell lots of people about their experiences and then consider seeking legal redress.

Americans should simply refuse to accept shoddy products or service.[1] When you have a negative marketplace experience, make sure your complaint does the most good. To be an effective complainer, you must first decide on the objective of the complaint. If your objective is to be treated a little better while in a store, just ask to see the person in charge. This may be the store manager or an assistant manager. Simply report the quality of service you received and request that someone more capable be provided so you can spend your money in the store. If your objective is to remedy a wrong, more work is necessary.

Table 8-1 shows the five sequential levels of complaining: (1) to business, (2) to manufacturers, (3) to self-regulatory groups, (4) to consumer action personnel, and (5) to the private-action legal arena. You can follow these channels individually or simultaneously, but it is important to begin with the seller.

Sequential Levels to Bring Your Complaint	Sequential Channels for a Complaint
1. Local business	Salesperson → supervisor → manager/owner
2. Manufacturer	Consumer affairs department → president and/or chief executive officer (CEO)
3. Self-regulatory organizations	Better Business Bureau → county medical societies → consumer action panels (CAPs)
4. Consumer action agencies	Private consumer action groups → media action lines → government agencies
5. Small claims or civil court	Small claims court → civil court

TABLE 8-1 Complaint Procedure—Sequential Levels and Channels

Note that federal agencies, such as the Food and Drug Administration, Consumer Product Safety Commission, and Federal Trade Commission, are not included in this table. These agencies can register consumer complaints, but they do not have the power to resolve individual consumer problems. Complaining to federal government agencies helps them obtain information to take collective actions against sellers.

Complaints about services should follow the same channels. Each type of service provider (i.e., doctors, chiropractors, lawyers, nursing homes, telephone bills, landlords, tax collectors, pre-schools) has an overseeing self-regulatory body and/or government agency. Appropriate addresses and telephone numbers can be obtained by looking in the front pages of the telephone directory and the blue pages listing government agencies.

---

[1] It is often reported in the popular press that the Germans and Japanese would never accept the quality of goods that most Americans do.

1. The Local Business

The best approach in complaining is to give the seller every opportunity to right the wrong before taking additional action. For example, a complaint about an unsatisfactory product, such as a faulty Panasonic telephone, should be brought to the attention of the merchant. Take the telephone back and talk to a salesperson. If he or she cannot resolve the problem, simply ask to see the supervisor. If you still get no satisfaction, such as a refund, a substitute product, or a repair, ask to see the manager or owner.

2. The Manufacturer

When a problem with a product cannot be resolved satisfactorily directly with a merchant and/or the difficulty is really with the product itself, you can keep your complaint about the merchant's lack of cooperation within the business self-regulatory scheme by bringing it to the attention of the manufacturer's consumer affairs department. Some companies, particularly automobile manufacturers, have a consumer affairs department **zone office** to respond to complaints. This is a corporation's decentralized geographic arrangement of consumer affairs office operations throughout the country to handle complaints. Both the zone and central corporate offices of consumer affairs should be equally able to resolve all difficulties.

A growing number of companies, particularly product manufacturers, provide toll-free telephone numbers for consumer inquiries and complaints. When a consumer experiences dissatisfaction at the merchant level, he or she can telephone the company. Addresses and telephone numbers of companies can be found on warranties, owner's instruction manuals, product hang tags, or in the library. Check *Standard and Poor's Registry of Manufacturers* or *Thomas' Registry of Manufacturers*.

CONSUMER UPDATE:
To Accurately Address Complaints, Use the
Consumer's Resource Handbook

The federal government's U.S. Office of Consumer Affairs publishes the *Consumer's Resource Handbook* every year. In addition to offering tips on buying smart, it provides thousands of addresses in a consumer assistance directory format. Included are corporations, national consumer organizations, car manufacturers, Better Business Bureaus, trade associations, government consumer protection offices, aging offices, banking authorities, insurance regulators, securities administrators, utility commissions, vocational and rehabilitation offices, weights and measures offices, selected federal agencies, and military commissary and exchange offices. Single copies are available free by writing: Consumer's Resource Handbook, Consumer Information Center, Pueblo, Colorado 81009.

Should you get no resolution from a senior-level manager in the consumer affairs department (don't take "no" from a low-level person!), then it is time to communicate with the manufacturer's president or chief executive officer (CEO). Simply send a complaint letter addressed to the title "President" or "Chief Executive Officer" and await the response. Chapter 14 explains and illustrates how to write a complaint letter.

3. Self-Regulatory Organizations

The role of self-regulatory organizations is to attempt to resolve disputes between consumers and sellers. Should the particular business, manufacturer, or profession not resolve the consumer complaint, then it's time to use sources of assistance outside the business. These are often called **third-party complaint-handling sources**. For example, county medical societies have judicial committees that handle written complaints, usually concerning overcharging or improper treatment, against member physicians.[2]

One major self-regulatory organization is the Better Business Bureau (BBB), which has offices in nearly 200 communities. The Better Business Bureau typically has four functions: (1) to provide prepurchase information to the public on such topics as "Tips on Buying a New Car", (2) to handle inquiries by providing reports to consumers on hundreds of local sellers, (3) to mediate disputes between consumers and businesses by accepting consumer complaints, forwarding them to the business involved, and encouraging settlement between the parties, and (4) to arbitrate disputes between consumers and participating sellers, often automobile manufacturers.

Consumers can obtain a number of useful booklets on consumer topics by visiting a local Better Business Bureau office. Those interested in learning about the reputation of any business in the country need only telephone the local Better Business Bureau where the company is located to obtain an oral report. Consumers wanting to complain about a seller must do so in writing to the BBB, which then mails a copy to the company, allowing 15 days for a response. Most sellers then tell the BBB their side of the story, which the BBB then presents to the consumer for reaction. Often a compromise settlement is reached between the consumer and the company. This is called **mediation**, which is the process of resolving or settling differences by acting as an intermediary agent between two or more conflicting parties. Companies that do not respond to complaints or mediate in bad faith can lose their membership in the Better Business Bureau. Consumers with unresolved problems can still take their complaints to a government consumer protection agency, small-claims court, or an attorney.

Arbitration is a method of having a dispute between two or more parties resolved by the judgment of an impartial person who is knowledgeable in the area of controversy. Many organizations, particularly trade associations, are involved in the arbitration of consumer disputes, such as the New York Stock Exchange, National Association of Securities Dealers (NASD), Chrysler Customer Arbitration Board, and local Better Business Bureaus throughout the country. Arbitrators are appointed by mutual consent of the parties involved or by statutory provision. The consumer almost never has to pay a fee for arbitration services.

The BBB has entered arbitration contracts with most automobile manufacturers, as well as other companies. Typically, a consumer who has complained to an automobile dealer about some problem usually also complains to the zone or head office of the manufacturer. When disputes still cannot be settled, the consumer can then ask the BBB through its Automobile Consumer Action Panel (AUTOCAP) to step in on the matter. In an arbitration case, the BBB hears the oral arguments of the consumer and the manufacturer and then makes a decision. Typically, the decision is binding on the

---

[2]In 1994, the Federal Trade Commission gave the country's medical societies the legal authority to discipline physicians for fee gouging when it occurs with other fraudulent or unprofessional behavior. Medical societies also may publicize such actions.

manufacturer but not binding on the consumer. Thus, a still dissatisfied consumer, if he or she desires, may go further and sue in court or ask a government agency for assistance.

In addition to the self-regulatory Better Business Bureaus, several industries have established **consumer action panels (CAPs)** to facilitate handling of complaints on an industry-wide basis. These are complaint-handling boards of impartial people, usually sponsored by an industry trade association, whose purpose is to mediate or arbitrate disputes between consumers and manufacturers or dealers. The usual 5 to 11 people who serve on CAPs are executives from a specific industry plus some consumer representatives. When the consumer action panel receives a complaint from a consumer, it asks the manufacturer or dealer to reinvestigate and report back. The typical CAP generally has the arbitration authority to make a decision that is binding on the business, but the consumer can accept or reject it.

Complaining to self-regulatory groups gives them the last opportunity to get the business to resolve the problem. Very often these groups can bring about a solution to a problem because they can be more objective than individual manufacturers or dealers, and such agencies have high success rates in resolving consumers' problems. For example, the car dealer's consumer action panel AUTOCAP resolves over 40 percent of its complaints in favor of car owners. When a problem cannot be handled by the local business, the manufacturer, or a local self-regulatory organization, consumers may contact one of the many consumer action panels or trade associations. See Chapter 15 for specific names and addresses.

4. Consumer Action Agencies

Consumer action agencies are third-party public and private organizations that purposefully and forcefully represent the interests of consumers, often by accepting individual complaints and taking action to resolve such problems. There are three common types of consumer action agencies: (1) media, such as newspapers, radio, and television stations, (2) government, such as county and state offices of consumer affairs and attorney general offices, and (3) private, such as local, state, and national consumer activist organizations.

In many communities the media is actively involved in consumer protection. A number of local newspapers and radio and television stations have "Action Line" programs whose purpose is to take actions to resolve a variety of problems concerning the public. Sometimes it is getting a pothole fixed on a busy street; often it is a consumer problem. When a consumer's effort has failed to solve a problem, the action line staff investigates and tries to right the wrong. An example of a media action line is Call for Action which is a network of radio and television stations that offer resolution for consumer problems. Call for Action's national office is located at 3400 Idaho Avenue, NW, Suite 101, Washington, DC 20016.

After being contacted by a media action line, many sellers quickly give in to the consumer's position because they fear the possibility of negative publicity. Typically, media staff are quite limited in the number of complaints they can investigate. As a result, they usually select complaints that are representative of the consumers' problems and often a bit sensational.

Government consumer action agencies include various consumer affairs offices and the offices of the attorneys general. Usually the Office of Consumer Affairs (OCA) is a state responsibility operating under the legal authority of the Attorney General's office.

Typically, government consumer action agencies run public service announcements on radio and television to solicit consumer problems, and they have toll-free telephone numbers for consumers to obtain complaint forms. Government consumer action agencies are located in the state capital with branch offices in major cities. In some instances, large cities and counties have their own offices of consumer affairs. Telephone numbers for state and local government consumer action agencies are listed in the front pages of the telephone book. These organizations have a high success rate in resolving consumer complaints because they can bring civil and criminal actions to enforce the laws and regulations, and they sometimes get fines and money back for consumers.

Private consumer action organizations exist everywhere. Local consumer action groups are just some of the many special-interest organizations trying to achieve their ends, such as helping senior citizens, improving access to low-income housing, and trying to preserve the environment. State and local consumer action organizations are usually well known to the populations they serve, such as the Consumer Education and Protection Association in Philadelphia and the California Consumers Association. At the national level, particularly active private consumer organizations include the Consumer Federation of America, Center for Auto Safety, and National Consumers League.

5. Small Claims and Civil Courts

Seeking remedies through the first four channels in the complaint procedures in Table 8-1 can rectify almost all consumer complaints. If these procedures fail, it is possible that the matter can be pursued in the legal arena. A survey last year by the American Bar Association found that at least 40 percent of consumers confront a non-criminal legal problem every year.

Numerous civil matters are resolved in state and federal courts, and a written record is made of the happenings. Proceedings are completed with the assistance of attorneys, witnesses, a judge, and often a jury. Few people take consumer complaints to an attorney and file suit against a seller in the regular civil court system because it is quite expensive. Attorney fees vary but easily could amount to $500 or even $1,000 to take a simple case to court. Examples of cases that consumers probably should bring to civil court include a breach of contract situation for a $3000 faulty air-conditioning system, a $5000 shoddy remodeling construction job, or a landlord-tenant dispute over $1500 in rent. People with limited incomes can go to legal-aid societies, usually listed in the telephone book under "Legal Aid" or "Legal Services", for less expensive attorney fees.

Damages to Ask for When Suing

When consumers go to civil court for a breach of contract or deception lawsuit, they sue for damages or relief. To remedy the wrong, consumers ask the judge for assistance. If a criminal act also has occurred during the unfair or deceptive practice, it is incumbent on the state or federal agency to seek civil and criminal penalties. In addition to asking the judge to award attorney fees and court costs, alternative actions for plaintiffs that are available in most lawsuits include actual damages, incidental expenses, consequential expenses, punitive damages, rescission, restitution, reformation, and injunction.

(1) **Actual** or **compensatory damages** usually include out-of-pocket losses and the difference between the consumer's expenses and the value claimed by the seller. This usually includes payment for mental anguish, physical pain and suffering, and various incidental and consequential expenses.
(2) **Incidental expenses** are those which result because of minor concomitant circumstances.
(3) **Consequential expenses** are those costs which the consumer incurs following as an effect, result, or conclusion of the unfair or deceptive trade practice.
(4) **Punitive damages** are those which aim to penalize or inflict punishment.[3]
(5) **Rescission** is the act of annulment or cancellation, as in canceling a contract. Rescission puts each party back into the position they were in before the unfair or deceptive practice occurred.
(6) **Restitution** is the act of restoring to the rightful owner something that has been taken away, lost, or surrendered.
(7) **Reformation** is the act of altering or correcting a contract, such as in removing faults or defects.
(8) An **injunction** is the act or instance of enjoining as it commands, directs, orders, or prohibits a party from a specific course of action.

Use a Class Action Lawsuit When Many are Wronged

Theoretically, the law protects consumers against frauds and misrepresentations, whether the case involves a Pepsi Cola overcharge of 5 cents, a $20 toaster, or a $20,000 automobile. The obstacles for redress are high for inexpensive items. It is difficult to prove deceit, and legal costs are significant given the expected small payoff. Thus, the pooling of grievances is sometimes allowed by the courts in the case of deceptions and misrepresentations through **class action lawsuits**. These permit representative members of a common class, such as consumers who have been similarly wronged, to seek joint redress of their grievances by suing for damages on behalf of themselves and all those similarly situated. Such lawsuits are usually permitted at the discretion of the state court where commonalities can be clearly shown.

Consumers who successfully file state or federal class action lawsuits may be awarded their purchase costs, attorneys fees, and damages. In addition, consumers injured by a breach of warranty may file a federal class action lawsuit. A class action lawsuit may be filed under the Magnuson-Moss Warranty Act if there are at least 100 named plaintiff-consumers each with a minimum claim of $25, and the total is at least $50,000. Few warranty problems meet all the restrictions necessary for consumers to economically and successfully pursue a class action lawsuit under the provisions of the Magnuson-Moss Act.

---

[3]In 1991, the Supreme Court refused to limit punitive damages, thus preserving a powerful tool for consumers to redress wrongs. Limits on punitive damages may be established by legislatures.

Alternative Actions for Consumers When Considering Breaking a Contract

When consumers receive goods that do not conform to the express or implied warranty, they can attempt to remedy the situation—break the contract—by: (1) keeping the goods and suing for damages, (2) rejecting of the goods, or (3) revoking acceptance and seeking a return of the purchase price. (Sometimes the consumer also can obtain consequential or incidental damages for the breach.) Most consumers do not choose to keep the goods and seek damages. Goods are sometimes rejected by consumers, but this requires fairly immediate action. In revocation, the consumer must fulfill a number of prerequisites because minor defects are not acceptable cause and consumers must give sellers an opportunity to cure the difficulty. Revocation must occur within a reasonable amount of time after discovering that a problem with the product substantially impairs the value of the item to the consumer.

CONSUMER UPDATE:
Auto Sales Contracts—Read Before Signing

Not reading a contract before signing it is a classic example of what can go wrong for consumers.

A third class petty officer asked her commanding officer on board USS YELLOWSTONE for advice on how to break the car contract she had signed a day earlier. After thinking about it for almost 24 hours, she concluded that she couldn't afford the payments. While she had negotiated for a $240 monthly payment, the "Good Boy Letter" sent to the command was asking for confirmation of a $360 allotment. She had mistakenly signed the contract before any of the figures were put in.

Immediately referred to the Command Financial Specialist (CFS), the petty officer could not produce the contract because the salesperson refused to give her a copy until he had the allotment in hand. The CFS made a telephone call to the 1-800 number for the state government Office of Consumer Affairs. The agency recognized the dealership as one with chronic consumer complaints and suggested that as a last resort the consumer, "Take the car back and leave the keys on the salesperson's desk. Then say, 'Have a nice day!'" The Office of Consumer Affairs person added that, "The worse they can do is sue!"

Attempting negotiation first, the CFS contacted the dealer and pointed out the fact that there was no copy of the contract proving ownership. After exchanging some dead-end comments on this unusual way of doing business, the CFS drove over to the lot with the petty officer. Since the salesperson still would still not produce the contract, he was left with the car. The threat that, "You can't do that!" prompted the CFS to call the state Lawyer Referral Service.

The lawyer contacted had some pending cases against the dealer and was happy to take the additional case. The cost for writing a "lawyer letter" revoking the petty officer's acceptance of the automobile was $100, but it succeeded in getting her out of the contract. She concluded that it was the best $100 she ever spent. Knowing that she should have read the contract and avoided all the mess, she then promised the CFS that in the future she would read all contracts before signing and to obtain a copy of all such documents. The petty officer was fortunate to have the CFS help her right a wrong using a little military consumer savvy.

*Jim Pressler, Hull Technician Chief, U.S. Navy

Chapter 8: How to Resolve Consumer Problems

> **CONSUMER UPDATE:**
> **Yes! You Can Get Out of Many Contracts***
>
> It is easy to give into the persuasive powers of a salesperson and sign on the dotted line of a contract. Later you may conclude that you should not have obligated yourself. Getting out of a contract depends upon (1) an appropriate federal or state law, and (2) the goodwill of the seller.
>
> **Automobile purchases and leases**—You usually can cancel if you have not yet taken possession of the vehicle, before the paperwork for the title gets processed at the department of motor vehicles, before you have put more than 5 or 10 miles on it, or before the loan or interest rate has been approved. Auto leases are almost impossible to cancel.
>
> **Insurance policies**—Most states permit a free cancellation period of 10 days; some allow 30 days to change your mind. Nationwide sellers are usually lenient. Follow correct cancellation procedures described in the fine print of the policy. Thus, you may be able to cancel life, health, disability, and credit insurance policies.
>
> **Extended Service Contracts**—These contracts almost always have a cancellation clause, typically 15 to 60 days. Most can be canceled later with a nominal service charge.
>
> Various federal and state "cooling-off laws" (described in Chapter 5) permit cancellation of contracts for health spas, campground contracts, home improvements, and timeshares.
>
> *Some of this material is based on Dan Moreau, You Signed it. Are You Stuck? *Kiplinger's Personal Finance Magazine*, October 1993, 53-56.

Use Small Claims Lawsuits to Sue When Necessary

For reasons of cost and convenience, many people choose to use small claims courts to resolve consumer problems. A **small claims court** (or **pro se court**) is a court specializing in adjudicating legal claims involving small amounts of money in a simple and economical manner, with relaxed procedures and rules of incidence, sometimes without the assistance of attorneys. Fully one-fourth of the total civil caseload in the United States is made up of small claims actions. Almost all states have small claims courts, and many courts are open during evening hours as well as weekends. The maximum amount that can be litigated is usually limited to $1200, although a number of states have a jurisdictional limit of $5000 or higher. Nine states permit jury trials.

Costs are kept low, in part, because a written transcript is not kept of the proceedings, although court records are maintained. In most small claims courts, consumers are prohibited from bringing an attorney into the courtroom. The idea is that the consumer can present his or her own legal claim before a judge in an informal setting, as some of the more formal legal proceedings are relaxed. The seller-defendant is usually allowed to have an attorney, although they are prohibited in some states. On most military bases and college campuses, free legal assistance is available to offer guidance on small claims cases, as well as other legal issues.

> **CONSUMER UPDATE:**
> **Rental Car Company Violates Human Rights Law**
> A 24-year old George Washington University law student successfully sued Hertz Rent A Car in small claims court for not renting a car to her. Pamela Sosne had an excellent driving record. However, rental car companies generally will not rent to people under age twenty-five without a hefty surcharge because statistics show that young people have more accidents than other age groups. Hertz does rent to people ages 21-25, but only if they are employed by a firm that has a contract with them. Sosne was awarded $101 in compensatory damages under the District of Columbia Human Rights Act which prohibits discrimination in the sales of goods or services. The only defense for a company is to show the court that they would be forced out of business unless they discriminated. Many cities have similar laws.

To file a small claims court action, you would go to the courthouse and inquire as to which court hears small claims. A small fee, often $10, is required, along with fees of normally $3 for each court summons or subpoena. A **summons** is a notice issued to a person summoning him or her to report to court as a juror or witness. A **subpoena** is a legal writ requiring appearance of certain items in court. When you complete the necessary forms, it is important to fill out the full legal name of the **defendant** (the person who allegedly committed the wrong act and is the subject of the litigation), and to carefully describe the action with which the lawsuit is concerned. The court will subpoena all necessary witnesses and the defendant for the day of the trial. The legal summons has a motivational effect on many defendants, since about one-quarter of all small claims cases are settled out of court before the hearing date.

The day the case is heard, you, the **plaintiff** (the person who has filed the small claims or civil court case and is suing the defendant), should be well prepared and have a clear understanding of the sequence of events that led up to the claim. Bring all relevant documentation. In most courts, the decision of the judge can be appealed by the loser to a higher court, which results in considerable attorney fees and related costs. Small claims court decisions are won by the plaintiff about three-quarters of the time and are not appealed.

Winning a small claims decision does not mean that you automatically get full satisfaction. Often the judge makes a compromise decision, perhaps ordering a $300 judgment on a $400 claim. Also, it is sometimes difficult to actually collect from the defendant. The small claims court does not act as a collection agency, rather it issues **judgments**. These are judicial decisions and determinations of a court of law, often creating or affirming an obligation, such as a debt.

If you experience difficulty collecting, you can go back to small claims court to ask the judge to order a **writ of execution**, which is a right to exercise a claim against the defendant's property, bank accounts, personal property (such as a motor vehicle), and wage income. Executions on real estate are not allowed. Going to small claims court takes time and energy, so consumers must weigh the potential benefits of going to court against the potential costs.

Chapter 8: How to Resolve Consumer Problems

Techniques of Last Resort: How to Fight Back—And Win!—Against Deceptive Practices

Virtually all consumers have been ripped off. When you have been deceived, you can fight back using these procedures:

(1) Review the deception and look for actual illegal actions by the seller. Think about suing the perpetrator in small claims court. Many college students enjoy the advantage of having a **student attorney** on campus. These persons are attorneys who are employed by the educational institution to attend to many of the legal interests of the student body. They generally give advice and guidance on legal issues, but occasionally a student attorney will file suit on behalf of a concern affecting one or more students. Low-income consumers, including most students and some military, can seek the assistance of legal-aid attorneys. When there is a lawyer involved, the complaining consumer has greater leverage when carrying on the fight because attorneys offer the appearance that the consumer is quite serious about the matter.

(2) Calculate the numbers to determine the likely value that a seller might settle for to get rid of your complaint. Sometimes it is important to obtain a full refund, so you should push for it. In other cases, 100 percent may not be necessary. Therefore, when seeking redress, it is important to know the likely value that a seller might settle for to get rid of your complaint. To begin, know that commissions for door-to-door and telemarketing sales are often 1/3 to 1/2 the sales price, in contrast to 5 to 10 percent for retail sales commissions.

To illustrate the process, assume the bad transaction cost you $200. The salesperson may have earned $80 commission on the deal, while the cost of the product or service may have amounted to a genuine $70 or so, leaving a gross profit to the seller of $50. Most sellers are willing to give a complaining consumer the salesperson's commission, plus part of the gross profit. Consequently, when communicating with a seller, calculate how much you are willing to compromise and how much wiggle room the seller probably has to settle the complaint.

(3) Fight back with multiple actions. Tell the seller that unless he or she meets your reasonable demands, that you will soon take a whole host of actions. After you have been nice, polite, and forceful, yet the seller remains unwilling to accommodate your interests, communicate that you are prepared to do the following:

- **Sue in small claims court** on the legal basis of **unconscionability** ("it was patently unfair, your honor, the seller took advantage of me") because any judge can rule so on the merits of a single case;
- **Make a big sign and picket the place of business** of the seller or where the seller goes to visit potential customers (avoid slanderous and libelous words and keep moving and you will break no laws);
- **Prepare a handout on consumer ripoffs** and distribute it to people you see while you are picketing (be careful from a legal perspective not to precisely disparage the seller in a slanderous and libelous manner), and share the handout with all your friends, too;
- **Write to the Attorney General, Office of Consumer Affairs, and Better Business Bureau;**
- **Offer to give speeches on consumer ripoffs** to any group that will listen;

- **Write press releases and letters to the editor**;
- **Write media action lines** for local newspapers and television stations;
- **Send the facts and story to the author of this book**, who will consider running it as a boxed insert in the next edition.

(4) Offer them a deal which they very well may accept.
After you have taken a few of the steps above, contact the seller again. Quietly communicate that it is in their best interest to compromise with you, one individual consumer, because the trouble you have caused and are going to cause them is costing them sales and may cost them morein the future. Tell them that for, "X" dollars, you will walk away satisfied. If not, tell them that you have all the time in the world to continue

---

CONSUMER UPDATE:
How to Organize a Boycott

One should use a boycott as a last resort. The *National Boycott News* recommends the following considerations: (1) Consider your target (the industry leader, the worst company, the one most likely to change); (2) Write the company explaining your position and seek a face-to-face meeting with a company official; (3) Should discussions prove fruitless, announce that you are considering a boycott and that you will continue negotiations over a list of demands that you present to the company; (4) Choose which company products to boycott and seek the cooperation of other groups which will support the boycott while sending the company names of boycott co-sponsors; (5) Call a press conference (if possible, at a company site) to distribute your list of demands and use graphic visual aids to help make your points.

---

to pursue your rights and that you will fight back! Either way, you will gain enormous satisfaction. And it is highly likely that you will win!

Chapter 9

Laws on Sales Transactions

Uninformed consumers often lose in marketplace transactions. All too often they pay too much for goods and services, they purchase products of inferior quality, and sometimes they suffer the consequences of unsafe products and illegal discrimination. Informed consumers similarly find themselves occasionally losing in the economic marketplace because the place where consumers meet sellers is difficult and challenging for all. Fortunately, there are a number of federal, state and local laws and regulations that serve to protect consumers and help them remedy marketplace wrongs. Most of these laws do more than provide disclosure. In addition, they empower consumers by giving them legal rights to take action. This chapter focuses on sales transactions regulated by federal and state laws, and it offers an occasional reference to local ordinances.

Laws and Regulations on Sales Transactions

A number of key laws and regulations in the area of sales transactions are described below, including: (1) Telephone Solicitations Regulations of the FCC, (2) Telephone Solicitation Laws of States, (3) Telemarketing FTC Regulations, (4) 900-Number Federal Communications Commission Regulations, (5) Unordered Merchandise Regulations of the Postal Service, (6) Negative Option Mail-Order Rule of the FTC, (7) Mail-Order Merchandise Regulations of the Federal Trade Commission, (8) Shopping by Telephone, Fax, and Computer, (9) COD (Cash on Delivery) Rule of the Postal Service, (10) Door-to-Door Sales Regulations of the Federal Trade Commission, (11) Door-to-Door Sales Cooling-Off-Period State Laws, (12) Cooling-Off Laws for Health Spas, Timeshares, Campground Contracts, and Mortgage Refinancing, (13) Refunds Accompanying Cancellation of Contracts, (14) Airline Bumping Regulations, (15) Airline Lost Luggage Regulations, (16) Pet Lemon Laws, (17) Travel Club Laws, (18) Weight-Loss Center Laws, (19) Customer-Owned Coin-Operated Telephone State Laws, (20) Rent-to-Own Laws, (21) Deliveries and Installations Laws, (22) Testimonial Advertising Guidelines of the Federal Trade Commission, (23) Comparative Price Advertising Laws, (24) Truth-in-Ticketing Package Tour Rule, and (25) Wheeler-Lea Act on Deceptive Advertising.

Telephone Solicitations Regulations of the Federal Communications Commission

The Federal Communications Commission has issued regulations to comply with the Telephone Consumer Protection Act of 1991. Rules cover unsolicited telemarketing solicitations, "junk fax", and auto-dialer calls. Telephone solicitations are banned between 9 p.m. and 8 a.m. All recorded sales pitches to consumers' homes are prohibited, unless the consumer gives permission to, or has a business relationship with, the company.

Callers must identify themselves and give an address or telephone number at which they or their company can be reached. A consumer who does not wish to receive telemarketing calls is required to tell each caller to place his or her name on the company's "do not call" list. That request must be respected for 12 months. Companies must get a consumer's approval before selling that person's telephone number to another marketer. The law gives consumers the right to sue marketers in small claims court for $500 to $1500 per violation. Enforcement of the law is given to the Federal Trade Commission, the Federal Communications Commission, the state attorneys general, and consumers themselves.

State Laws on Telephone Solicitation

Some states have more stringent laws regulating unsolicited telephone calls. For example, Kentucky prohibits automated calling equipment solicitations unless: (1) the recipient consents, (2) the call terminates within 10 seconds of denial or consent, (3) the caller is identified during the first 25 seconds, (4) the call does not involve random dialing, and (5) the solicitation effort may not occur between 9 p.m. and 8 a.m.

Also, a few states permit consumers to cancel goods ordered by telephone from a solicitor. Such states have **cooling-off rules** that apply to telephone sales which permit consumers a certain number of days to change his/her mind and cancel a contract. These laws generally require that the telephone solicitation seller forward the consumer a contract confirming the order and that the contract is not valid until returned with the consumer's signature. More information on cooling-off laws is below.

FTC Telemarketing Sales Regulations

There are an estimated 700 telemarketing firms in the United States who employ between 3 and 5 million employees in this multi-million dollar industry. They make at least 18 million calls per day, therefore, every U.S. household receives at least one telemarketing call each week. Unfortunately, about ten percent of the telemarketers are not legitimate.

The Federal Trade Commission has national standards that govern telemarketers. The FTC established rules in 1993 to implement part of the Telephone Disclosure and Dispute Resolution Act. More recently, the FTC issued additional telemarketing sales rules as required under the 1994 Telemarketing and Consumer Fraud and Abuse Prevention Act; the newer regulations went into effect December 31, 1995. All these rules are designed to help protect consumers against deceptive and abusive telemarketing sales practices. Following are the several provisions of these laws.

Calling times are restricted to the hours between 8 a.m. and 9 p.m.

Before they make their sales pitch, telemarketers must "promptly" tell you that it is a sales call, provide the name of the seller, and tell what they are selling. However, telemarketers are allowed to delay telling the purpose until they have established "rapport" with the call recipient.

If the pitch is for a prize promotion, they must tell you the odds of winning and that no purchase or payment is necessary to enter or win. They also are required to tell you any restrictions or conditions of receiving the prize. It is illegal to misrepresent the value or nature of a prize.

It is illegal for telemarketers to misrepresent any information at all. In the area of telemarketing of investments, work-at-home, and business opportunity schemes, for example, it is illegal to misrepresent the facts about the goods or services, the earnings potential, profitability, risk, or liquidity.

Before you pay, telemarketers must tell you the total cost of the goods and any restrictions on getting or using them, or that a sale is final and nonrefundable. Telemarketers may not withdraw money from a consumer's checking account with express, verifiable authorization, such as in writing on paper or audiotape. Consumers are not required to pay for credit repair, recovery room, or advance-fee loan/credit services until such services are actually provided. Telemarketers are prohibited from lying to get consumers to pay, no matter what payment is used.

Also, it is illegal for consumers to help deceptive telemarketers if they know, or consciously avoid knowing, that the telemarketer is breaking the law.

Telemarketers are prohibited from calling you once you have requested to be placed on its "do not call" list. The consumer is the only person who can implement the protection. To do so, the consumer must take the trouble to explicitly inform the telemarketer that calls are no longer permitted. It is important to record in writing the date, time, company name, and the caller's name every time a telemarketing call is received. The list is valid for only 12 months, after which the telemarketers may call again. Furthermore, the "do not call" list is for individual products being sold, not the entire company's line of products. Violators are liable for up to $500 in damages per unwanted call and up to $1,500 in damages per willful violation. Consumers may sue telemarketers who break this law in their local small claims court; consumers also may ask their state attorney general to sue the telemarketers.

Many telemarketers participate in the Direct Marketing Association's "National Do Not Call List," as they have agreed not to telephone consumers who add their names to this list. To sign up, write Telephone Preference Section, Direct Marketing Association, P.O. Box 9014, Farmingdale, NY 11735-9014.[1]

The strongest provision of the 1995 regulations is that state law enforcement officers, such as the attorney general, now has the power to prosecute fraudulent telemarketers who operate across state lines by suing in federal courts. State officials are allowed to get nationwide injunctions that will prevent an unscrupulous seller from moving operations to another state. State governments will no longer have to chase fraudulent telemarketers from state to state. Instead, such businesses will be shut down entirely. Fines are $10,000 per violation, and consumers are supposed to receive restitution of losses suffered. The new regulations do not preempt stronger state laws where they exist.

Some weaknesses remain in the telemarketing sales rules. In particular, if the telemarketer chooses to not mention its refund policy as part of its sales offer, such information need not be provided the consumer. The biggest weakness is that the telemarketing caller is permitted to avoid telling the purpose of the call until he or she has established rapport with the person called. That leaves too much time for the unscrupulous telemarketers to lure the consumer into a web of deceit. The regulations also do not prohibit courier pickups of payments or the use of unsigned checks without first getting explicit authorization from consumers.

Other moral rights are also provided to consumers in telemarketing transactions. Consumers have the right to request the telemarketer to mail written information about the investment, charity, product, service, its cost (including yearly cost, such as for magazines), and guarantee. You also have the right to ask whether the caller is a professional telemarketer/fundraiser or a volunteer.

900-Number Federal Communications Commission Regulations

The Federal Communications Commission issued rules in 1993 to implement part of the Telephone Disclosure and Dispute Resolution Act. Consumers who do not want calls made from their telephones to 900-numbers (pay-per-call services) must be given a block on their telephones. The consumer's local telephone company must list the charges for pay-per-call services separately on the customer's bill.

All pay-per-call services costing more than $2, either on a flat-fee or cost-per-minutes basis, are required to begin with a **preamble**, a message disclosing the price and the identity of the company providing the service. They must sound a warning signal telling the consumer that he or she has only three seconds remaining to hang up before another tone begins that lets the caller know the paid service is beginning. Callers must be permitted to hang up early and not be charged. Services aimed at children under age 12

---

[1] If you want to remove your name from most mailing lists to receive less advertising mail, write Mail Preference Service, Direct Marketing Association, P. O. Box 9008, Farmingdale, NY 11735-0998.

are prohibited; services directed to 12- to 18-year-olds must state that parental permission is needed to complete the call. Companies must provide a local number or a toll-free line to call with billing questions.

Ads for 900-numbers must meet certain disclosure standards. Advertisements in print or broadcast media are required to provide specific pricing information, consisting of reporting charges for service options callers might select.

Rules for settling disputes are similar to credit card regulations. Billing complaints must be acknowledged in writing within 40 days and resolved within 90 days. The 900-number companies, or their representatives, have 90 days to eliminate the disputed charges or investigate and demand payment. A consumer's credit rating cannot be penalized until the dispute is addressed. Consumers should complain first to their local telephone company because it is authorized to resolve disputes; an oral communication is sufficient notice to initiate a billing review. If requested, the local telephone company will provide a written explanation and copies of any documentary evidence of the consumer indebtedness.

CONSUMER UPDATE:
Fight Back Against Ripoff Telephone Charges

Shockingly large telephone bills can be caused by fraud, ripoffs charges of alternate operator services (AOS) and coin-operated customer-owned telephones (COCOTS), use of 900- and 976-numbers, calls made by unattended children, and long-distance billing errors. Don't put up with such charges. Instead, complain to your local telephone company and ask them to credit your account.

Although the rates of non-traditional telephone companies are generally not regulated, consumers who are ripped off may challenge any and all excessive charges to their local telephone companies. Even though the local telephone company did not cause the problem and is not responsible for its solution, complaining consumers usually get some relief. Local telephone companies are required by law to do the billing for other firms that provide services to their customers. The contract typically states that, "Contested charges by consumers will be charged back to the original service provider." As a result, local telephone companies are inclined to give in to consumer complaints. Ask for a supervisor, if necessary.

Unordered Merchandise Regulations of the Postal Service

Federal regulations of the U.S. Postal Service state that if you receive merchandise in the mail that you did not order, you may consider it as a gift. You are under no legal obligation to pay for it or return it. Postal Service regulations specify that you do not have to pay for unordered merchandise and that it is illegal for the company to bill you for it or send you dunning communications for unordered merchandise. In fact, the only materials that can be mailed to you without your permission are those clearly marked as free samples and merchandise mailed by charitable groups asking for a contribution. Even in these cases, you can consider any merchandise as a gift. Of course, you cannot keep something like a video cassette recorder inadvertently mailed to your home. If you are sure the merchandise was never ordered, write the company that you are keeping it as a free gift. Say you are sending a copy of your letter to the Office of Consumer Affairs, and do so. Keep a copy for your records.

The unordered merchandise regulations state that you can refuse a shipment that arrives by U.S. mail simply by not opening it and returning it to the post office. By writing "Refuse to accept" on a package and giving it back to the post office, it is returned to the sender at no cost to the consumer.

If you are not certain that you ordered goods that have arrived by U.S. mail, consider sending the company a letter (preferably certified with a return receipt requested) and ask for proof of your order. If you get unordered merchandise by private delivery services, such as UPS or Federal Express, do not accept the shipment. If you have already accepted it, write the sender a certified letter and get a return receipt. Demand proof of your order. If there is no valid proof, tell the sender that unless the merchandise is picked up within 30 days, you will dispose of it. If you return it, be sure you do so at the sender's expense and get a receipt from the carrier.

Negative Option Mail-Order Rule of the Federal Trade Commission

Books, records, compact discs, videotapes, and other items are often sold through membership in a negative-option club. Typically, the consumer receives an introductory offer, such as three books for $1, if you agree to purchase more items. A **negative option** is a consumer decision-making situation in which the consumer must notify the company that a particular selection is not desired in order to not receive it, because if the company does not receive the negative notification, the consumer will receive the goods according to the previously agreed-to contract.

The FTC Negative Option Rule requires that sellers clearly and conspicuously give consumers certain information about the plan in any promotional material. For example, the seller must tell: (1) how many selections you must buy, if any, (2) how and when you can cancel your membership, (3) how to notify the seller when you do not want the selection, and (4) when to return the negative option form to cancel shipment of a selection. The regulation requires that the company give consumers at least 10 days to reject the monthly or periodic selection, based upon the **mailing date** (the date the form must be postmarked to the seller) or the **return date** (the date the form must be received by the seller).

Mail-Order Merchandise Regulations of the Federal Trade Commission

The FTC has a trade regulation concerning mail-order merchandise sales. The regulation requires that (1) the buyer should receive any ordered merchandise when the seller promises to deliver it, such as within three weeks, unless the advertisement promises a different shipping time, (2) when no date is mentioned, the seller must ship the merchandise no later than 50 days (before this year this was 30 days) after receiving the order (evidenced by receiving the payment, charging a credit account, or getting the telephone order [the last part is a proposed regulation]), and (3) if the consumer does not receive the ordered merchandise by the 50-day deadline, the order can be canceled and the consumer can get his or her money back. The 50-day clock does not begin until the order is received. At least one part of the transaction must take place through the U.S. mail in order for the rule to apply.

The seller has specific responsibilities if the promised delivery date (or 50-day limit) cannot be met. The seller must communicate to the consumer with an **option notice** the new shipping date and give the consumer the option to cancel the order and obtain a refund or agree to a new shipping date. If paid by charge or credit card, the seller has one billing cycle to credit the account. A free means of response must be provided, such as a postage-paid postcard or a toll-free telephone number. If the consumer fails to reply and if the delay will be less than 50 days, the company can assume the consumer agrees to the delay. For delays over 50 days, money must be refunded to consumers who have not given their consent to such a delay. Prepaid orders that are canceled must be refunded within 7 days.

If you have received the notice and have agreed to a new shipping date, the company must notify you if it cannot deliver by that date. You once again have the opportunity to respond to the company that you either accept the extended shipping date or want a refund. The company must cancel the order and refund your money if you do not sign and return the second notice.

These regulations cover a number of mail-order situations for consumers, mostly affecting transactions with traditional mail-order firms. However, there are exceptions to the rules: mail-order photo finishing; magazine subscriptions; serial deliveries (such as negative-option plans, as in book and record clubs), except for the initial shipment; mail-order seeds and plants; COD (cash on delivery) orders; and credit orders that are not charged until the goods are shipped. Note that the regulations do cover orders placed by telephone and paid for by mail.

Refunds for orders paid by check, money order, or cash must arrive at the consumer's mailing address within 7 business days of the merchant's receipt of the cancellation. For credit-card orders, the consumer's account must be credited within one billing cycle. The FTC defines a **business day** as Mondays through Saturdays, not Sundays or the Mondays following a national holiday.

Shopping by Telephone, Fax, and Computer

The mail-order merchandise regulations of the Federal Trade Commission (described above) apply to shopping by telephone, fax and computer. Effective last year, the FTC regulations safeguard the right of consumers to exercise the option of canceling orders and receiving refunds for goods that cannot be promptly delivered. A seller must ship telephone, fax and computer orders within the time stated in its advertisements. If no time is promised, the company should ship your order within 50 days of receiving it (formerly 30 days). Otherwise, the company must give you the choice of agreeing to a delay or canceling the order and receiving a prompt refund.

COD (Cash on Delivery) Rule of the Postal Service

Rules were issued by the U.S. Postal Service in 1987 that provide that people may pay for COD packages with a check made out to the mailer instead of the Postal Service. This option enables consumers who experience difficulty with mail-order merchandise to

> **CONSUMER UPDATE:**
> **Free Magazine Trial Subscriptions that Keep on Coming**
> A consumer responds to a promotion for "one free magazine trial issue" and doesn't like the publication. A month later the bill comes and the consumer marks the bill "please cancel" before returning it. Then another magazine arrives, then another bill, and it goes on seemingly forever.
> To get out of these magazine contracts, send the latest bill back with a short letter telling them that you responded to the trial offer and, according to their original terms of offer, you attempted to cancel the subscription by returning the first bill marked accordingly. Write that you do not want a subscription and you are not paying for the issues received. In general, minors under the age of 18 can disavow contracts, such as for magazines, and their parents or legal guardians cannot be held responsible. Simply write to the company and explain the circumstances.
> These companies are too busy soliciting new subscribers, so they always give in to an effective consumer demand. With "hardheaded" companies (i.e., not too many people working there who want to properly serve consumers), contact the Magazine Publishers Association, 919 3rd Avenue, 22nd Floor, New York, NY 10022 (212-752-0055) and request that the magazine company stop billing you. If necessary, send the magazine company a bill of your own for $5 for storage charges for the unwanted magazines.

stop payment on a check before it is cashed. Then the buyer will only be out the bank fee to stop payment on the check.

It is important to recognize that mail frauds have not gone away. Consumers are still allowed to give cash, money orders, and certified checks to the U.S. Postal Service for COD packages sight unseen. In short, now consumers have the right to pay COD charges to the seller or to the Postal Service. Uninformed consumers may not realize that the new U.S. Postal Service regulation exists and, therefore, may not exercise their right.

Door-to-Door Sales Regulations of the Federal Trade Commission

The Federal Trade Commission (FTC) has a trade regulation under the Truth in Lending Law regarding door-to-door sales. It provides something called a **cooling-off period**, which is a time period during which the consumer has the opportunity to reconsider the wisdom of making a door-to-door contract purchase, change his or her mind, cancel the contract, and obtain a refund.

The FTC door-to-door regulation applies to sales agreements for $25 or more made anywhere except in the seller's normal place of business. Therefore, consumers can cancel agreements for $25 or more made in motel rooms, restaurants, their homes (including dormitory rooms), and the homes of friends or acquaintances. The rule generally applies whether the consumer invited the seller into the home or the seller made the arrangement. The cooling-off period also applies when your home is used to secure the loan no matter where the contract was signed. The FTC regulation does not apply to sales made entirely by mail or telephone, for emergency home repairs, maintenance or repairs on personal property, arts and crafts sold at fairs, for purchases of insurance, securities, or real estate, or for sales made at the seller's normal place of business.

The FTC regulation states that consumers have the right to cancel most door-to-door contract purchases (both cash or credit transactions) within 3 days of the original purchase. The FTC regulation requires that on door-to-door sales of $25 or more, the salesperson must verbally tell consumers of this right to cancel a contract, give the consumer a written contract, and give the consumer two copies of a "notice of cancellation," that must be in the same language used in the sales presentation.

The law requires that the notice accompanying the contract be dated, show the name and address of the seller, and include the following statement: "You, the buyer, may cancel this transaction at any time prior to midnight of the third business day after the date of this transaction. See the attached notice of cancellation form for an explanation of this right." Consumers have until midnight of the third business day after the contract date to cancel. To do so, the consumer either: (1) dates, signs, and mails the form to the address given for cancellation, being sure to retain one of the detachable copies of the cancellation form and getting the envelope properly canceled with the correct date by the Postal Service, or (2) hand delivers it to the same address. If necessary, consumers can make their own cancellation form letter as long as it provides the same types of information found on the proper cancellation form.

The seller has several responsibilities to perform within 10 days if a consumer cancels a sales agreement: (1) cancel and return any contract papers signed, (2) refund any money and return any trade-in, and (3) tell the consumer how and where the product not desired will be picked up or returned.

Within 20 days, the consumer must make available to the seller the item to be returned, and it should be in the same condition as when it was received. The consumer must pay return shipping charges if he or she agrees to do so. Alternatively, the seller might agree to pick up the item and/or pay for the return shipping expenses.

Door-to-Door Sales Cooling-Off-Period State Laws

There is no general three day right to cancel all contracts. Most states have their own cooling-off period laws that extend the protections offered in the FTC regulation for door-to-door sales. States often allow consumers to cancel sales contracts made for any amount, including those under $25, if the agreement was made away from the seller's regular place of business, such as in the consumer's home or in a motel suite. The contract must have been for personal or household purposes. Most states provide that such contracts can be canceled by midnight of the third business day (Saturday usually counts as a business day). To cancel, follow the instructions on the cancellation form provided as part of the contract. Most states require notice of contract cancellation in the same language as the oral presentation. Some states have specific statutes that allow cancellation of magazine contracts sold door-to-door.

Cooling-Off Laws for Health Spas, Timeshares, Campground Contracts, Mortgage Refinancing, Etc.

Many consumers are pressured into signing contracts on the spot, in order to take advantage of a one-day-only deal. Most states have specific cooling-off statutes for particular types of contracts no matter where the agreement was signed, in someone's home, in a motel suite, or at the seller's place of business. In general, cooling-off laws permit the consumer to reconsider his or her action and exercise a penalty free cancellation of an agreement after thinking about the situation for three to fifteen days. There is no need for any justification. Laws generally require that the consumer receives notification of the right in writing from the seller. A written notification of cancellation must be delivered by certified mail, return receipt requested, or by personal delivery, to the address on the contract. If delivered in person, the consumer should have an employee acknowledge in writing receipt of the cancellation. Consumers should always keep a copy of any cancellation notice. Other contracts you can cancel under various state laws include dance lessons, seminar sales, dating services, discount buying clubs, hearing aids, rental housing locators, trade and correspondence schools, foreclosure sales, home repairs, martial arts, condominium sales, and multiple magazine subscriptions.

Refunds Accompanying Cancellation of Contracts

Many states have laws permitting consumers to change their minds months after signing contracts with sellers. In such instances, the law typically specifies the proportion of the refund available for the unused portion of the contract. Reasons for cancellation vary. In Virginia, for example, a consumer can cancel a health spa contract should one become unable to use the facilities for health reasons. Further, you can cancel if the spa location you had been using closes and another one is not within five driving miles of the former location. Some states permit contract cancellation from health spas should you move your place of residence more than 25 miles. (For more information on which contracts may be cancelable, see Chapter 8.)

Consumer Leasing of Automobiles

The Consumer Leasing Act was passed in 1976 to protect consumers who lease automobiles. It covers leases for personal or household use that are longer than four months when the total obligation is less than $25,000. It requires that the leasing company disclose to consumers written information about payments, taxes, title, licensing fee, insurance, warranty, who will pay for maintenance and repairs, and how the purchase price will be calculated if the lease has an option-to-buy provision. The law does not require the leasing company to provide a "capitalization" cost figure, which is the number one needs to properly compare leasing to buying.

Airline Bumping Regulations

Airlines often cancel or delay flights because of mechanical problems, bomb threats, and inclement weather. However, the sole legal obligation of an airline company is to place the passenger on its next available flight to that persons' destination. Also, there are no regulations requiring that airlines assist a consumer if a flight is missed because the passenger was late. Wise consumers do ask for, and often get, a voucher good for travel on a future flight. And, when delayed overnight, many airlines will pay for a hotel room and a meal or two. Usually, only assertive consumers who ask get such assistance.

Department of Transportation (DOT) rules do exist for overbooking problems. If your flight was overbooked and no one volunteers to give up a seat, the last one on is usually the first to get bumped. The U.S. Supreme Court ruled last year that passengers bumped from oversold flights may sue for compensatory (not punitive) damages for actual injuries in a state court.

Should you be involuntarily bumped, you are not entitled to reimbursement when the airline is able to get you to your destination by means of any airline within 1 hour of your scheduled arrival time. Beyond 1 hour but less than 2 hours (4 on international flights), assuming you met the airline's check-in requirements, the airline must pay you a cash penalty. The amount must equal the one-way fare to your final destination up to $200. If you are more than 2 hours late, the airline must pay you twice the amount of the ticket up to $400. If this happens to you, make sure that the alternate ticket is for a confirmed seat, not standby, because you may get bumped again. Many airlines provide up to $25 in cash or vouchers for food and miscellaneous expenses when a flight is seriously delayed. People who volunteer to be bumped (four-fifths of the total) usually receive a voucher for a free domestic round-trip ticket, sometimes some cash, have a few hours delay at the airport, and continue to their destination on a later flight.[2]

Even though most airlines may compensate consumers with cash for free meals, telephone calls, and other minor necessities in these situations as a gesture of goodwill, you may have to ask for the number and call the consumer affairs office of the airline to get help. In addition, when your baggage is delayed or lost, most airlines will provide courtesy bags containing toiletries and give you up to $25 in cash or vouchers for miscellaneous expenses, but usually only if you ask. Complaints about airline service may be made to the Department of Transportation (202-366-2220).

Airline Lost Luggage Regulations

Department of Transportation (DOT) regulations specify that the airlines have a maximum liability for lost or damaged luggage of $1850 on domestic flights and a maximum of $920 on international flights. However, the regulations do not say what has to be covered. As a result, policies among the airlines vary. Most airlines do not accept any liability for lost computers, cash, jewelry, camera equipment, or similar valuables. When your baggage is delayed or lost, most airlines will voluntarily provide courtesy bags containing toiletries and give you up to $25 in cash or vouchers for miscellaneous expenses.

Pet Lemon Laws

Several states require dog sellers to disclose facts about the animal's health to the purchaser in writing, including health, age, and history. California requires sellers to reveal what state the dog came from, whether obtained from a licensed or an unlicensed dealer, its immunization record and health information. New Hampshire requires sellers

---

[2]No such regulations exist for hotels and motels, even reservations guaranteed with credit cards and confirmation numbers. A breach of contract situation exists when a hotel tries to turn a consumer away who has confirmed reservations, therefore, insist to the manager that he or she book you elsewhere and pay for the room.

to show prospective buyers a health certificate for both dogs and cats. Animals usually can be returned within one or two weeks of purchase; animals suffering from congenital disorders may have up to one year to be returned.

Some states (AR, CA, CT, FL, NH, NY, VT, VA) also have laws that allow consumers to return an unhealthy dog to the seller for a refund, another animal, or payment of veterinary expenses to cure the animal. Consumers are entitled to the cost of veterinary services used to determine the animal's health status or to relieve its suffering. Alternatively, consumers may be entitled to another animal plus some veterinary expenses. Those who want to keep their unhealthy animal are entitled to receive reimbursement for limited and reasonable veterinary expenses.

Travel Club Laws

A growing number of states are passing laws to protect consumers who pay fees to join travel clubs. For example, last year a Virginia law went into effect that requires travel clubs to pay an annual registration fee of $350 and a $60,000 bond as proof the firm will deliver on its promises. Virginia consumers are given a seven-day cooling-off period during which they can cancel the agreement.

Weight-Loss Center Laws

Some states and localities have statutes to regulate weight-loss centers. For example, New York City's law requires four steps: (1) commercial weight-loss centers must post a prominent "Weight-Loss Consumer Bill of Rights" sign in rooms where sales presentations are made that inform consumers there may be serious health problems associated with rapid weight-loss, and that only lifestyle changes (such as eating healthful meals and regular physical activity) promote permanent weight-loss, (2) weight-loss centers must hand out the bill of rights to potential clients, (3) centers must disclose the hidden costs of products or laboratory tests that may be part of the program, and (4) weight-loss centers are required to tell dieters the duration of their recommended program.

Customer-Owned Coin-Operated Telephone State Laws

A number of states have begun to regulate customer-owned coin-operated telephones. Often consumers are faced with having no choice but to use a coin-operated telephone that is not owned by the local telephone company, rather it may be owned by the business upon whose property it is located. Common problems include excessive charges to alternate operator services (instead of using the services of the well-known local and long-distance telephone companies), restricted access to long-distance carriers, and prohibitions on using 911 for emergencies.

Some state regulators are requiring that customer-owned coin-operated telephones must: furnish local directory information (at a reasonable rate, such as 30 cents), provide a dial tone, provide free calls to 911, have a surcharge for long-distance calls (such as, "AT&T plus 10 percent") if the information is posted on the phone, be hearing-aid compatible, and not charge more for local calls than the rate already approved for traditional telephone companies.

Rent-to-Own Laws

In an effort to stop consumers from being overcharged, a number of states have passed laws regulating aspects of rent-to-own contracts.[3] In New York, for example, consumers are allowed a 7-day "cure" period to make delinquent payments and/or redeem an item that has been repossessed. This action reinstates the original contract with credit for all previous payments. If partial payment is made along with voluntarily returning the merchandise, the reinstatement time period can be extended up to 180 days.

New York also requires: (1) disclosure of the cash price of an item, (2) the price of the rental option, and the total price (a combination of the first two, which cannot be more than 100 percent greater than the cash price), and (3) the information must be attached to each displayed item. Amounts assessed for late charges are limited, and consumers are allowed to buy the rented item at any time for the cash price less one-half the total of previous payments. Further, if advertising mentions the possibility of ownership, the total cost of the option must be given. Since many rent-to-own companies operate nationally, there is interest in legislation at the federal level.

Deliveries and Installations Laws

Some states protect consumers from having to wait at home for hour after hour for deliveries and installations that never happen or occur quite late. California, for example, requires a maximum delivery-installation time period of four hours for cable television companies, utilities, and business firms with 25 or more employees.

Testimonial Advertising Guidelines of the Federal Trade Commission

Endorsements and testimonial advertisements encourage consumers to think that the advertised message is honest. The Federal Trade Commission advertising guidelines require that testimonials or endorsements always reflect the honest opinions, findings, beliefs, or experiences of the endorser; that the endorser continues to subscribe to the views presented; and that, if asked, the advertiser can substantiate the endorsement. Further, when payment of promise of compensation might materially affect the credibility of the endorsement, that connection must be disclosed.

---

[3] An excellent summary of the problems associated with rent-to-own buying can be found in: Swagler, R. & Baschon, C. (1989). *Advancing the Consumer Interest*, 1, 30-31.

Comparative Price Advertising Laws

Many state and local governments regulate comparative price advertising to reduce deceptions and misrepresentations. The law in Virginia, for example, forbids sellers from advertising "former" or "comparative" prices for merchandise unless the store can substantiate the facts. If a seller compares a price to that of another seller's price, the claim must meet three tests: (1) it is the actual price of another seller, (2) the trading area from which the price comes must be identified, and (3) it is clear that the price is another seller's price.

In Virginia, if the price in an advertisement is compared to a previous price, the claim must satisfy one of four tests: (1) it is the price at which substantial sales took place, (2) the price is offered in good faith, (3) the former price was based upon customary markup practices, or (4) it includes the date on which the item was sold at the former price. Although auto dealers in Virginia are exempt from the law, it has reduced the use of such terms in advertising as "manufacturer's suggested retail price" and "list price" in department store and other retail advertising.

Truth-in-Ticketing Package Tour Rule

The Truth-in-Ticketing Package Tour rule of the U.S. Transportation Department went into effect in 1994. It affects any tour organized for the purpose of attending a sports, social, religious, educational, cultural, political, or other event for which admission is advertised as part of the tour. The law provides that tour operators must have a substantial number of tickets on hand or under contract before they may advertise a tour package. Tour package firms are prohibited from accepting payment from an individual consumer unless an actual ticket is available or they have a firm contract for the ticket. Such firms must refund a tour customer's money within three days of the booking if no ticket is available. Also, the price of the tour may not be increased within ten days of the trip. And, if any price increase is more than ten percent, the consumer must be allowed to cancel and receive a full refund.

Wheeler-Lea Act on Deceptive Advertising

The Wheeler-Lea Act of 1938, and its further amendments, is aimed at stopping misleading claims in advertising and labeling. This law covers all consumer products. The law prohibits false, deceptive, or misleading advertising and labeling. An unwillingness to state pertinent facts about the product is considered misleading advertising. The Wheeler-Lea Act is a key legal tool of the Federal Trade Commission in fighting various types of consumer frauds and deceptions.

Chapter 10

Laws on Credit

There are a number of extremely powerful laws that protect consumers in credit transactions. But when not used, all the laws and regulations in the world will not help resolve a single consumer problem. One credit law says that you can "charge back" certain "unsatisfactory" goods when purchased on credit. Really! Read on, get empowered, and use the credit laws to protect you, your family, and your friends.

Laws and Regulations on Credit

A number of key laws and regulations in the area of credit are described below, including: (1) Limited Liability on Credit Cards, (2) Electronic Funds Transfer Act, (3) Automatic-Billing Disputes, (4) Fair Credit Reporting Act, (5) Fair Credit Billing Act, (6) Equal Credit Opportunity Act, (7) Holder-in-Due-Course Doctrine, (8) Fair Debt Collection Practices Act, (9) Fair Credit and Charge Card Disclosure Act, and (10) State Laws on Credit Card Disclosures, and, (11) Home Ownership and Equity Protection Act.

Limited Liability on Credit Cards

The Fair Credit Reporting Act, passed in 1972, limits the liability for unauthorized use of credit cards, including telephone credit cards. It results in a maximum liability of $50 per card. This **credit-card liability** occurs only if you receive notification of your potential liability, you accepted the card when it was first mailed to you, the company provided you with a self-addressed form with which to notify them if the card was lost, and the card was used illegally before you notified them of the loss. If you notify the credit-card company within two days of a lost or stolen card, you are not legally responsible for any charges; after that time period you are liable for only $50 in false charges. In addition, there is no time limit for reporting unauthorized charges when someone has illegally used your credit card; however, you must specify in a complaint letter to the credit card company that it is an "unauthorized charge."

Although your financial liability is low, some companies specialize in selling lost credit-card insurance; it is profitable for them and an unnecessary expense for you. Besides, consumers who have renter's or homeowner's insurance typically have coverage that automatically protects them against such losses. Further, as a gesture of goodwill, most companies waive the $50 fee for unauthorized use of credit cards. As might be expected, the credit-card insurance companies generally do not offer such information.

Electronic Funds Transfer Act

People often make regular "direct deposits," such as a paycheck, stock dividends, or Social Security benefits, to financial accounts electronically. You also can authorize your financial institution to pay recurring bills in both regular amounts (such as a mortgage or automobile loan) and irregular amounts (such as for electric or telephone bills). Federal law permits you to stop a pre-authorized payment by calling or writing the financial institution, so that your new order is received at least three days before the payment date. Written confirmation of a telephone notice to stop payment may be required by the institution.

The Law Applies to Electronic Transfers, Debit Cards, and Credit Cards Used as Debit Cards

All kinds of electronic transfers occur daily for most consumers. Federal and state regulations have been adopted to provide protection for EFT users. (Electronic benefit transfers are currently exempt from the EFT regulations, since most electronic benefits programs are experimental.) The 1978 Electronic Funds Transfer Act is the governing statute and the Federal Reserve Board's "Regulation E" provides the specific guidelines on EFT-card liability. The Electronic Funds Transfer Act affects consumer use of electronic transfers, debit cards, and credit cards used as debit cards.

Rules specify that a valid card can be sent only to a consumer who has requested it. Unsolicited cards can be issued only if the card cannot be used until validated and the user is informed of liability for unauthorized use as well as of other terms and conditions. When you sign up for EFT services, your depository institution must inform you of your rights and responsibilities in a written disclosure statement containing the above information.

Consumers get written receipts when withdrawing money or making deposits with an ATM machine or using a point-of-sale terminal to pay for a purchase. These show the amount of the transfer, the date it was made, and other information. General protection of customers' accounts exists in the form of a periodic statement that financial institutions regularly send out. These show all electronic transfers to and from your account, any fees charged, and the opening and closing balances. EFT users should regularly reconcile the information on their periodic statement with the written receipts.

Correcting Errors on Periodic Statements

Should you find an error in your periodic statement, notify the issuing organization in writing as soon as possible. Correct notification procedures can be found in the disclosure statement. You have 60 days from the date of the statement or receipt error to notify the financial institution, otherwise the institution has no obligation to investigate. Always telephone and follow up with a letter. If the institution needs more than 10 business days to investigate and correct a problem, generally it must return to your account the amount in question while it finishes the investigation (within a required 45 days). If there was an error, the institution must correct it promptly by making the correction final. If there was no error, the institution must explain in writing why it believes there was no error and let you know that it has deducted any amount temporarily credited during the investigation. However, the institution must honor withdrawals against the credited amount for 5 days. You may ask for copies of documents relied on in the investigation and again challenge if a mistake has been made.

Lost EFT Cards

The sooner you report a lost electronic funds transfer (EFT) card, the more likely you will limit your liability if someone uses your card without your permission. Cardholders are liable for only the first $50 of unauthorized use if they notify the issuing company within 2 business days after the loss or theft of their card or code. Between 2 and 60 days, cardholder liability for unauthorized use rises to $500. If you fail to alert the financial institution within 60 days, you risk *unlimited* loss. Thus, you are liable for every dollar stolen in your account, plus your maximum overdraft line-of-overdraft credit. The logic is that if cardholders examine their monthly statements, they will note unauthorized use of the account. These regulations are for specific EFT cards *and* for other cards used to make an electronic funds transfer (such as a Visa credit card). A number of states have laws that provide additional protections for consumers in EFT transactions.

It is difficult for consumers to dispute an item with a merchant (for faulty goods, for example) if the merchant has already been paid by means of EFT. Because the merchant already has the money, the consumer's only recourse to correct or reverse EFT transactions is to ask for a refund.

DID YOU KNOW?
Your Present Homeowner's/Renter's Insurance Covers the Liability for Lost Credit and Debit Cards

Many companies sell specialized liability insurance in a separate policy for an annual premium of $30 to $60. In addition, some firms sell a **card registration service** that will notify all companies where you have debit and credit cards in the event of loss. For $15 to $50 a year, you only need to make one telephone call to report all card losses. Alternatively, in case of loss, you can notify debit and credit card companies yourself.

Realize, too, that homeowner's and renter's insurance policies typically cover the liability for the unauthorized use (usually theft) of both debit and credit cards. If not currently protected, such insurance coverage generally can be added to a homeowner's or renter's policy for $10 to $15 a year.

Automatic-Billing Disputes

As a matter of convenience, many consumers give their credit card or checking account number to vendors so that regular monthly fees may be automatically charged, or debited, to their accounts. If charges come directly out of a checking account, a problem may occur because your money is gone and it is hard to get it back.

Consumers do have protections from *electronic* debits to their bank accounts under the Automated Clearing House (ACH) rules governing financial institutions. After receiving a statement, consumers have 15 days to tell their bank that the charge was unauthorized. It is then the bank's responsibility to prove the validity of the charge, or reverse the debit. However, there are no protections for consumers for *paper* debits. Alternatively, if you permit charges to a credit card, you have the protections of the Fair Credit Billing Act (discussed below) that allow consumers to dispute an unauthorized charge up to 60 days after it occurred.

Fair Credit Reporting Act

Most credit reporting is done by **credit bureaus**, which compile information about credit applications and forward it to the creditor. A creditor comes under the Fair Credit Reporting Act only when credit information from one firm is forwarded to another and a credit decision is based on that information. The objective of the act is to place certain restrictions on credit-reporting agencies to reduce errors.

Rights Exist If You Are Denied Credit

If you are denied credit because of a poor credit report, the law requires disclosure to you of the name and address of any credit-reporting agency that supplied information about you. You can then request a summary of the contents of your file at the credit-reporting agency without a fee; a cost-free credit report must be requested within 30 days of denial. If you dispute an item, it must be reinvestigated. If the information was in error, it must be corrected. You also may wish to tell your side of the story on a disputed item by adding, in 100 words or less, a **consumer statement** to your credit file (see an example of a "consumer statement" in Chapter 14). All such information (corrections or your side of the story) must be sent to anyone who received a credit report on you in the previous 6 months.

All Consumers Have the Right to Know the Contents of Their Credit File

Even if you have not been denied credit, for a small fee (usually about $5 to $15) you can obtain a copy of your credit bureau file. A credit record may be retained for a period of 7 years for judgments, liens, lawsuits, and other adverse information except for bankruptcies, which may be retained for 10 years.

If you have applied for life insurance or employment, a credit bureau might compile an **investigative report**. These are much more detailed than regular consumer credit reports. They often involve interview comments from neighbors and friends about your lifestyle, morals, character, and reputation. For these kinds of investigative reports, you must be informed when a report is being compiled.

DID YOU KNOW?
How to Get a Copy of Your Credit Report for Free

Most of the more than 2000 local credit bureaus belong to national groups that have access to credit histories of over 80 million people, such as Equifax (P.O. Box 740256, Atlanta, GA 30374-0256; 800-685-1111), Trans Union (P.O. Box 7000, North Olmsted, OH 44070; 800-851-2674), and TRW Credit Data (P.O. Box 2350, Chatsworth, CA 92313; 800-422-4879). TRW gives consumers a free report once a year, just for the asking. Nice company policy, TRW!

Fair Credit Billing Act

The Fair Credit Billing Act (FCBA) went into effect in 1975 to establish procedures for the prompt correction of errors on open-end credit accounts. It provides safeguards against unsatisfactory purchases and uncooperative merchants. The law also protects a consumer's credit rating while the consumer is settling a dispute. In the past, complaining about a credit card bill often resulted in delays and in harmful information going into a consumer's credit file.

Under the claims and defenses portion of the law, also known as the **charge back** section, consumer's may legally withhold payment for a disputed amount for a number of reasons. Consumers may not be responsible for a charge on their credit account if it:
 (1) is in error,
 (2) was not made by a person authorized to use the account, or
 (3) is for goods and services that were not provided or delivered according to agreement, or in other words they were "unsatisfactory".

To exercise these rights and force the credit card issuer to "charge back" the amount in dispute,[1] a consumer must notify his/her credit card issuer in writing indicating that he/she is disputing a particular charge on the account and give the reason. This challenge must be done within 60 days of receiving the bill that contains an error, unauthorized charge or has a charge later found to be unsatisfactory. A telephone call to the lender will not preserve your rights.

The credit card issuer must investigate such inquiries and respond in writing within two billing cycles. During the time when the company is looking into the problem, consumers are not required to pay the questioned amount or pay any finance charges associated with the disputed amount. These rights do not guarantee consumers a refund, but the law does require that the credit card issuer investigate the matter in their effort to resolve the dispute.

With all challenges to credit card bills, if the credit card issuer turns down the challenge, the consumer still owes the amount of the charge, plus any finance costs that have accumulated (but were suspended until the challenge was resolved). However, any subsequent reports sent to a credit bureau must state that the consumer disputes the charges, and the consumer must be told who receives such reports for the following six months.

The law is limited to credit card purchases for over $50, which have not been paid for, that were made within your home state or within 100 miles of your home (whichever is farther). While this excludes overseas purchases, some U.S. credit card issuers have voluntarily extended the coverage around the world. In practice, most credit card companies allow consumers to contest any disputed amount, regardless of amount or distance from one's home. With telemarketing transactions, a consumer can easily make the case that the purchase occurred inside his or her home. In addition, the seller may have placed advertisements in the local media which, of course, would be within 100 miles of the consumer's home.

If the consumer has already paid the card issuer for a charge before realizing that a problem existed, one's legal leverage has been lost; however, most issuers are willing to work with customers who have been ripped off. Moreover, making payment with a credit card offers consumers much more protection than when paying with cash or a check.

The FCBA also states that bills must be mailed to cardholders at least 14 days before payments are due. Companies are required to send a reminder of their consumer credit rights under the FCBA to all customers twice a year. Another provision requires that retailers who voluntarily give price discounts of up to 5 percent to cash customers must

---

[1] These rights exist both in the United States and overseas, although in some foreign countries local laws may limit one's FCBA rights.

publicly state that information. In this way, cardholders can choose to elect to pay cash and thus avoid the extra costs the merchant imposes on credit accounts.

Consumers Get to Keep $50 of the Disputed Amount if the Credit Card Company Fails to Follow the Rules

Failure of the company to follow all the rules within the proper time limits, the law allows the cardholder to keep the first $50 of the amount in dispute, even if it is money the consumer owes. Alternatively, the consumer may sue for damages resulting from the violation, plus twice the amount of any finance charge (not less than $100 or more than $1,000), plus attorney fees and costs.

Reason #1 to Challenge a Credit Bill—Consumers Are Not Liable for the Errors of Others

If the credit card company discovers that an error has been made, the consumer is not liable for the charges in dispute, for any minimum payments, or for finance charges that apply to the amount challenged. Examples of billing errors: (1) an amount different from the actual purchase price, (2) arithmetic mistakes you later discover on the merchant's sales slip which makes the total incorrect, (3) failure to reflect a payment or a credit for merchandise returned, (4) something you simply do not recognize as having purchased, (5) something about which you want additional clarification because it is confusing and perhaps not clearly identified on a bill (i.e., place, description, date), and (6) something not accepted on delivery. A sample complaint letter challenging a credit card bill is shown in Chapter 14.

After investigating a challenge, the credit card issuer typically forwards the complaining consumer a photocopy of the signature on the credit slip. The issuer's position often is, "Well, if that is your signature, you still owe us the money, so stop your complaining and pay us what is owed." Consumers should not be taken in by such an attitude and quickly give in and pay the disputed amount. If it is your signature, but there is some genuine problem with the bill, write the card issuer again reaffirming the challenge. This time write to a supervisor at the credit card issuer, being even more explicit with your explanation. A sample complaint letter to a supervisor at a credit card company is shown in Chapter 14.

Another good reason to challenge an "error" is that the credit card bill was received too late or not received at all. This problem often occurs when people move from one address to another and when the Postal Service loses the mail. In this instance, the consumer simply writes to challenge the finance charges that were incorrectly imposed on the account. Such charges should be credited on the account provided the lender received notice of that new address at least 20 days before the end of the billing period.

If the credit card issuer disagrees with and rejects the challenge, they must tell the consumer why they believe the bill is not in dispute. At this point, the consumer may ask for copies of relevant documents and then refile the complaint (perhaps with more information). Refusal to pay may result in the lender beginning collection procedures, although credit card issuers usually do not begin to send collection letters for 90 days.

Reason #2 to Challenge a Credit Bill—It Appears to be an Unauthorized Charge

If your reason for the challenge is that the charge appears to be unauthorized, the card issuer will forward you a photocopy of the signature on the credit card slip so it can be examined. Should the consumer write back reporting that the signature is not valid, the credit card issuer must give in and accept the challenge as legitimate. That means that the challenged amount will immediately be credited. If the amount involved is substantial, the card issuer's fraud investigative unit will contact the consumer in an effort to obtain additional information that might be useful in investigating and catching the culprit who falsified the signature.

Reason #3 to Challenge a Credit Bill—Unsatisfactory Goods

Examples of unsatisfactory goods and services include: (1) ordered merchandise was not ever delivered to your home, (2) stitching in a new jacket ripped out under normal use, (3) fraudulent emergency auto repairs were made to your vehicle while on an out-of-town trip, (4) you did not enjoy a terrible meal at a restaurant about which you complained to the merchant, and (5) you lost a night's sleep in a noisy motel room where you complained to the night manager to no avail.

Key to successfully winning with dispute is that you *must* make a real attempt to resolve the problem with the merchant. Chapter 14 contains Illustrative letters that can be sent to the merchant and the credit card issuer. If you attempt to challenge a credit card bill on the grounds that you are dissatisfied without first, or simultaneously, contacting the merchant in an attempt to resolve the matter, the card issuer will very likely refuse your request and reinstate the charge to your account.

Moreover, consumers may challenge billing errors for defective or deficient products or services. If you use a credit card to purchase goods that are shoddy or damaged or receive poor quality services, the law protects you by giving you certain rights that may be exercised. In addition, the defective nature of the goods or services is a valid defense against any later lawsuit by a credit card issuer.

When Necessary, Consumers Should Write Firm Letters to Merchants and Credit Card Companies

To properly dispute a credit card charge, first, write the merchant to complain and, if appropriate, seek a compromise. Second, write a complaint letter to the credit card company. Provide the credit card company with a chronology and as much documentation as possible, so that they can contact the merchant to try to thrash things out. During that time creditors cannot send **dunning letters** (notices that make insistent demands for repayment) to you or send negative information about your account to a credit bureau without stating additionally that, "Some items are in dispute." Sample letters are in Chapter 14.

When writing, be pleasant but firm, state only the important details, and tell them what you want done. Many consumers wisely charge any and all expenses that might later turn out to be a problem, such as air travel and auto repairs while on trips. For travel expenses, the 60-day period to contest a charge begins from the date of the bill, not the date of travel. Last year three companies extended the challenge time for travel charges: Visa voluntarily extended the time period from the date of travel, MasterCard 120 days from the date of the bill, and American Express up to a year.

> **CONSUMER UPDATE:**
> **Sample Complaint Letters to Resolve Credit Problems**
> There are six sample letters in Chapter 14, and four deal with credit problems. Of those letters, one disputes an item on a credit card bill. The second complains to a merchant requesting credit for an unsatisfactory purchase. The third complains to the credit card issuer to obtain a credit for an unsatisfactory purchase. The fourth complains to a supervisor at a credit card issuer, and it is to be used if the credit card issuer turns down an initial request to dispute an item on a credit card bill.

Equal Credit Opportunity Act

Discrimination in lending against women, the elderly, and religious and racial minorities resulted in the passage of the Equal Credit Opportunity Act of 1975, which prohibits discrimination in granting credit. Rejecting a credit application due to poor credit history is legal, but rejecting a person on the basis of sex, race, color, age, marital status, religion, national origin, or because the person receives public assistance is not. It also prohibits discrimination because of good faith exercise of any rights under the federal credit laws and regulations. By law, credit applications cannot probe for information that could be used in a biased manner. The Equal Credit Opportunity Act requires creditors to provide to the applicant a written statement, if requested, of the reasons for refusing credit. Should discrimination be proven in court, the lender may be liable for up to $10,000 in fines.

Lenders must use the same criteria to judge applications from single and married persons. A married man or woman applying for credit need not disclose marital status or a spouse's income unless he or she is dependent on that income, in which case it is used as the basis for granting credit. Several states take exception to this, considering any property acquired by either the husband or wife, known as **community property**, as jointly owned and equally shared.

Holder-in-Due-Course Doctrine

The traditional **holder-in-due-course doctrine** held that if a merchant sold a product on credit to a consumer and then sold the credit contract to a sales finance company or other lender (the holder), a legally binding contract existed between the consumer and the lender. Should the merchant go out of business or simply refuse to repair a defective product, the consumer still had to pay the full amount owed to the holder. The only recourse for consumers was to sue the original seller (who usually was bankrupt); however, by law payments to the finance company had to continue.

The Federal Trade Commission, in a 1976 ruling with the force and effect of law, has almost eliminated almost all instances of this practice. In general, the FTC regulations permit withholding of payments to such third parties for defective products or services.

This is true for both credit-card and non-credit-card purchases. In addition, both the seller and the holder are legally responsible should the consumer sue for replacement of the product or for payments already made. For a defective product, it may well be the manufacturer that is finally legally liable. This protection, however, does not apply when the borrower independently makes the lending arrangements directly with a creditor.

Fair Debt Collection Practices Act

This 1977 legislation was aimed at eliminating abusive, deceptive, and unfair debt collection practices. It applies to third party debt collectors or those who use a name other than their own in collecting consumer debts. Banks, dentists, lawyers, and others who do their own collecting are exempt. **Collection agencies** attempt to make collections of debt from consumers that could not be obtained through the usual procedures of sellers. Under law, collection agencies may not harass debtors, telephone before 8:00 a.m. or after 9 p.m., make numerous repeated telephone calls during the day, misrepresent themselves (such as claiming they are attorneys, unless they are) or the purpose of their communication, make threats, make racial or ethnic slurs, use abusive language, or spread rumors that you are a "deadbeat". Collectors may not call the debtor at work if the agency knows such calls are not allowed. Even with these limitations, realize that collection agencies can be irritatingly persistent in collecting past-due accounts. If they are not successful, they take the consumer to court and seek a default judgment as the last resort.

Debtors have the right to tell a bill collector to have no further contact with them. Should the collector persist, debtors should write a letter and firmly inform the collector to stop. Should harassment continue, the debtor can report the law violations to the Federal Trade Commission, the state attorney general, and the local telephone company.

Fair Credit and Charge Card Disclosure Act

The Fair Credit and Charge Card Disclosure Act of 1988 provides that credit-card issuers must reveal a number of important pricing details before consumers sign up for the credit cards. The law requires any direct-mail credit application or solicitation to reveal: (1) the annual percentage rate (APR) of interest, including the way the rate is calculated and if the rate is variable, (2) the method used to calculate the monthly account balances against which the company applies interest or finance charges, (3) all fees, including annual fees, minimum finance charges, transaction charges, cash-advance fees, late fees, and fees for going over the credit limit, and (4) the length of time of the grace period, if any. Information such as APRs, annual fees, and grace periods must be provided in tabular form. Companies that impose an annual fee must provide disclosures before annual renewal. Card issuers that offer credit insurance must inform customers of any increase in rate or substantial decrease in coverage should the issuer decide to change insurance providers.

This law allows consumers to comparison shop for credit cards. Since research from the Survey Research Center of the University of Michigan indicates that about 35 percent of us shop for the most attractive interest rate on credit cards, a lot of Americans are able to use the information.

DID YOU KNOW?
You Can Refuse to Pay the Higher Rate When a Credit Card Company Raises Your Interest Rate

If a credit card company raises the interest rate on an existing account, the consumer has the right to reject any commitment to paying the higher rate. To do so, one must notify the card issuer in writing. By law, interest charges on the remaining debt must be at the old interest rate. Any continued use of the credit card means that the consumer has accepted the new higher terms.

State Laws on Credit Card Disclosures

Several states have laws requiring additional disclosures to credit card customers. In Massachusetts, for example, the law requires that credit-card users who have paid an annual fee who cancel their cards before their membership has expired are eligible for a partial refund. Also, all banks (including out of state) must notify cardholders in Massachusetts one month in advance of assessing an annual fee.

Home Equity Loan Consumer Protection Act

Recent data from the Federal Reserve Board reveal that 12 percent of all homeowners, about 7.5 million people, have established some type of home-equity loan. A **home-equity loan** is an open-ended credit plan secured by the borrower's principal residence. Some 40 percent of home-equity loans are used for home improvements, 30 percent are used to repay debts, and the remainder is used for new purchases. Less than 3/4 of 1 percent of such loans are delinquent, and this compares to 2 1/4 to 3 percent for other types of consumer loans. Borrowers can lose their homes if they do not repay their home-equity loans.

The Home Equity Loan Consumer Protection Act of 1988, Regulation Z of the Federal Reserve Board, and a 1994 mortgage disclosure regulation (see below) attempt to curb some of the abuses in the growing home-equity loan market by providing borrowers with more information about the costs of such loans. The regulations prohibit lenders from unilaterally changing the terms of a loan after a contract has been signed. It prohibits lenders from calling in loans before the due date, except in cases of fraud or misrepresentation by the borrower in connection with the loan, failure to meet the payment obligations, or borrower behavior that jeopardizes the value of the home.

Advertisements promoting initially low "teaser" rates must display the current long-term interest rate with equal prominence. Advertisements must include cost information, such as loan fees, the rate used to compute finance charges, the maximum

For variable-rate home-equity loans, lenders must link their interest rate formula to a public index outside the lender's control. They also must tell applicants the frequency

> **DID YOU KNOW?**
> **Why It is Difficult to Get Out of Secured Loans**
>
> A **secured debt** requires **collateral**, which is a certain asset that the borrower pledges to back up the debt. A loan secured with collateral means that the lender has a **secure interest** in that collateral, usually a motor vehicle, electronic equipment, furniture or appliance. Thus, in the event that the borrower fails to repay the loan, the creditor can repossess the collateral. **Repossession** means to reclaim physical control of the collateral goods for failure to repay credit installments. A clause used in almost all credit contracts to speed up the repossession process for lenders is the **acceleration clause**. This states that after one payment is late, the loan is in default and all remaining installments are due and payable at once or on the demand of the lender.
>
> The lender typically records a lien in the county courthouse in order to make the security interest known to the public. A **lien** is a legal right to take and hold property or to sell it for repayment of a claim. When the credit contract is paid in full, the lien is removed. Sometimes a loan is secured with the signature of a **co-signer**, another person who agrees to pay the loan should the borrower fail to do so. Co-signers have the same legal obligations for repayment as the original borrower; therefore, being a cosigner is a major responsibility.
>
> Lenders are not motivated to compromise on collecting secured debts because, one way or another, they expect to get their money back. Consumers who want to get out of secured debts might try to persuade the lender to take back the secured property and forgive the amount owed. Most lenders will not agree, but it is worth asking. Some lenders will take back the goods but only if the consumer is willing to offer some extra cash—up front—to persuade the lender to agree.

of changes in the annual percentage rate and provide a 15-year historical table showing how the rate and payments would have been affected by changes in the value of the index.

All borrowers must receive detailed information on the home-equity loans along with the credit application before any fees are paid. Lenders have to disclose information on interest rates, fees, interest ceilings, an estimate of fees imposed by third parties, and repayment options, and they must provide an example of a repayment schedule. Should any terms change before the loan is finalized, the consumer has the right to demand a complete refund of all fees paid.

Still legal are variable rates that may fluctuate widely, **balloon loans** in which regular monthly payments are followed by an extremely large lump sum payment of the balance, and **negative amortization** of a loan that allows the unpaid balance to grow rather than diminish. The latter occurs when the repayment amount received by a creditor is less than the amount of interest assessed during a given time period.

Most banks give you a special checkbook to access your home-equity loan. A number 1of credit-card companies in concert with banking institutions are offering home-equity loans with a credit card that can even be used at ATM machines. Therefore, every time the card is used, part of the equity in the cardholder's home disappears. Home-equity loans allow consumers to charge regular purchases, even impulse items, on their credit account. This service is being offered, in part, because interest on home-equity loans is deductible when calculating personal income taxes while other consumer interest is not. Many consumers are afraid of the temptation of being able to charge things against their homes. After all, misuse of a home-equity loan can put you right out of your home.

Chapter 10: Laws on Credit **115**

> **CONSUMER RIGHTS UNDER THE MILITARY GARNISHMENT LAW**
>
> It is now legal to garnish the pay of military service members when a creditor has obtained a valid judgment from a civilian court of law in the state where the debt exists. A **garnishment** is a legal proceeding whereby money or property due belonging to a debtor but in the possession of another is applied to the payment of the debt. Here the court directs a third party (in this case, the military) to withhold the money from one's pay and forward it to the plaintiff.
>
> The maximum amount that can be withheld is 25 percent of disposable pay or the amount allowed by state law, whichever is less. (The states of CT, ME, SC, PA, and TX will not allow garnishment except for family support.) Excluded from base pay are retired pay, retainer pay, separation pay (VSI or SSB), and allowances such as VHA and BAQ.
>
> Procedurally, the court-ordered judgment is sent to the Defense Finance and Accounting (DFAS) which forwards one copy to the service member and two copies to the person's commanding officer. DFAS can begin garnishment 30 days after the command responds, which has up to 90 days to respond to DFAS with the completed application.
>
> The Soldiers' and Sailors' Civil Relief Act (SSCRA) protects the rights of service members by postponing court proceedings if military duties prevent them from representing themselves. Therefore, garnishments will not be allowed if the service member was deployed or exercising military duties at the time of the proceedings. The commanding office makes the final determination as to this ruling. Once notified of a court judgment by DFAS through the commanding officer (who has five days to contact the service member), the service member has 15 days to seek legal advice.
>
> Thus, it is wise for service members to not let merchants or landlords get the upper hand, legally, in situations where there is a consumer problem or controversy. Service members are encouraged to challenge any court action taken against them (perhaps because he or she defaulted on a contract to purchase an automobile, neglected to repay a vehicle repair bill, or left a rental contract not paid) because, if unchallenged, such creditors are now capable of garnishing that service member's pay. Learn your consumer rights and responsibilities to avoid these dilemmas.
>
> *Paul Rubino, Financial Education Specialist, Navy Family Services Center, Norfolk, Virginia

Home Ownership and Equity Protection Act

The Home Ownership and Equity Protection Act (HOEP) of 1994 amends the Truth in Lending Act and aims to eliminate the unscrupulous practice of making predatory loans in the second mortgage market. Many homeowners, especially older, low-income, and minority consumers, have fallen prey to fast-talking salespersons who promise to finance home repairs, consolidate bills, or pay for other important expenses.

The way the scam works is that the financing uses the consumer's home as security for the high-cost, and often unaffordable, loan. As a result, the homeowner winds up spending regular income on high credit repayments. Within a short time period, the is unable to make the monthly payments. Next the person's home is lost through foreclosure or forced sale. Oftentimes, the financial institution that eventually causes the loss of the home is an historically reputable lender that had purchased the credit contract from the firm that originally financed the loan. In the meantime, the shady, high-interest-rate lender has absconded with the equity, often many thousands of dollars, in the home. This is a form of **reverse redlining** where, instead of ignoring neighborhoods of minorities and the poor, unscrupulous lenders intentionally target and victimize consumers in the communities where credit is often difficult to obtain.

The Home Ownership and Equity Protection Act discourages legitimate lenders from making such loans or buying credit contracts from the original holders of the notes. HOEP also provides new remedies for victims of such unethical practices.

The law creates new regulations for a particular type of closed-end loans. **Closed-end loans** are those with set payment terms, such as 60 monthly payments of $200. (This is in contrast to open-end loans where consumers can tap into a line of credit, like a credit card or a traditional home equity loan.) A loan that uses a person's home for security will meet the requirements of the law and be defined as a **special home-ownership closed-end loan** when one or more triggers occurs: (1) if the annual percentage rate (APR) of the loan is more than 10 percentage points above the yield on certain Treasury securities, and (2) the loan's upfront fees and charges are greater than 8 percent of the total amount of the loan or $400, or more. (Exempt from HOEP regulations are traditional residential mortgage loans, reverse mortgages, and open-end credit transactions.)

Lenders now must make a great number of disclosures regarding the terms of such loans, and they are prohibited from using certain terms and placing onerous conditions in their contracts.

When violations of the HOEP law occur, the victims of such high-interest loans have three *years* to cancel the transaction.[2] The borrower, of course, is required to give back the proceeds of the loan to the lender, however, all obligations to pay interest and closing costs are canceled. These claims may be made against the original lender as well as the current holder of the note. This recision right is expected to be a powerful influence in the market and, hopefully, force the reduction or elimination of such home-ownership closed-end loan scams.

---

[2]This right of recission is provided in the Truth in Lending Act, and it extends the historic three-day cooling-off period for some credit transactions.

Chapter 11

Laws on Vehicles

Consumers sometimes experience problems when buying or repairing vehicles. To avoid problems and get out of consumer difficulties when they occur, it is important to know your legal rights when purchasing new or used vehicles, as well as the laws and regulations on vehicles repairs.

Laws and Regulations on Vehicles

A number of key laws and regulations regarding vehicles are described below, including: (1) Odometer Fraud Laws, (2) Motor Vehicle "Buyer's Orders", (3) Lemon Laws for New Vehicles, (4) Used Vehicle Lemon Laws, (5) Used Vehicle Lemon Branding Laws, (6) Vehicle Repair Laws, (7) Secret Warranty Disclosure Laws for Automobiles, and (8) the Federal Trade Commission Used Car Rule.

Odometer Fraud Laws

Odometer fraud occurs when an odometer is rolled back or disconnected and when incorrect information is given about the accuracy of the odometer reading. The Federal Odometer Law requires that the odometer reading be entered on the vehicle's title in all states. Federal law permits consumers who are wronged by odometer fraud to sue the seller and, if they win, collect $100 in damages, plus attorney's fees.

Motor Vehicle "Buyer's Orders"

Several states have laws designed to stop dealer financing arrangements from being changed after the customer has agreed to a deal. The situation occurs when a purchaser contracts to buy a car, based on assurances that dealer financing will be obtained at a certain percentage rate. Perhaps a week later, after leaving the trade-in car behind, the dealer telephones saying that the financing rate is going to be several points higher, meaning much higher payments. Such contracts are binding in most states. A number of states now require that the sale of a car is not finalized unless the proposed sales contract is approved under the terms agreed to by the purchaser. The consumer can cancel the contract and require any down payment and/or trade-in be returned if anything specified in the contract is changed.

Lemon Laws for New Vehicles

A **lemon law** is a statute designed to assist vehicle purchasers who are experiencing major car defects or severe mechanical difficulties and/or are finding it impossible to get the vehicle repaired satisfactorily in a reasonable length of time. All states have such laws, and such authorities have been upheld by the U.S. Supreme Court.

The term was coined by Connecticut legislator John J. Woodcock III, who first came up with the "lemon law" concept to provide consumers with a remedy to their problems with defective cars. A **lemon** is described by Woodcock for consumers as, "a chronically defective vehicle that defies repair, or ... a vehicle with defects so difficult to diagnose and repair that the consumer becomes immersed in the wear-down process resulting in the new-car buyer throwing in the towel, after absorbing an emotional and financial beating."

More than 150,000 consumers every year face the problem that they purchased a lemon vehicle.

CONSUMER UPDATE: Getting Out of Vehicle Contracts

It is easy to give into the persuasive powers of a salesperson and sign on the dotted line of a contract. Later you may conclude that you should not have obligated yourself. Getting out of a contract depends upon (1) an appropriate federal or state law, and (2) the goodwill of the seller.

Automobile purchases and leases—You usually can cancel if you have not yet taken possession of the vehicle, before the paperwork for the title gets processed at the department of motor vehicles, before you have put more than 5 or 10 miles on it, or before the loan or interest rate have been approved. Auto leases are almost impossible to cancel.

Extended Service Contracts—These contracts almost always have a cancellation clause, typically 15 to 60 days. Most can be canceled later with a nominal service charge.

Most states legally define a **lemon** as a passenger vehicle meant for personal or family use that has been unsuccessfully repaired four or more times for the same problem that substantially impairs the use, value, or safety of the vehicle or the car has been in the repair shop for a cumulative total of 30 days during the first year. Lemon laws offer improved warranty protections to consumers. Report safety problems to the National Highway Traffic Safety Administration at 800-424-9393.

The lemon owner wants to return the car and get his or her money back or get a replacement vehicle because the problem is major and has reduced the use, safety, or value of the vehicle. This procedure is called **revocation of acceptance**. It is instigated by returning the vehicle to the dealer and writing a letter specifying why this action is being taken. This may be difficult for many consumers to accomplish; thus in states without lemon laws most consumers have to hire attorneys and sue in civil court to obtain redress. Some states, such as Virginia, provide that if the consumer wins in court, the consumer's attorney and expert witness fees shall be paid by the manufacturer. Since in many cases returning a vehicle may cause a hardship on consumers, lemon laws do not require lawsuits. In lemon law states, problems with the vehicle must occur within one year or during the length of the warranty period, whichever is shorter.

The typical lemon law provides that if a newly purchased car is in the shop for a total of 30 days during the first year of ownership (or 12,000 miles) or if the same problem is not successfully repaired after three or four attempts, the consumer is entitled to redress. The manufacturer usually has two choices: (1) refund the purchase price, including all collateral expenses (such as title fees, repairs, mileage to and from the dealer, sales taxes, inspections, and vehicle rental) plus money for loss of use of the original car, less a reasonable charge for the miles driven, or (2) replace the vehicle with a comparable model acceptable to the consumer.

Consumers exercising their lemon law rights must first exhaust remedies under a manufacturer's informal dispute settlement procedure before going to court. In these cases, the dealer or manufacturer usually has to pay the prevailing consumer-plaintiff's reasonable attorney fees (if any), expert witness fees, and court costs.

One provision of many lemon laws creates a state recovery fund that enables lemon vehicle buyers to collect court judgments against automobile dealers or salespeople. Even after winning a lawsuit, sometimes the consumer cannot collect because the defendant closes the business and/or leaves town. A state recovery fund typically requires that each dealer and salesperson be assessed $10 to $100 a year to create a fund out of which claims can be paid to consumers.

Used Vehicle Lemon Laws

Lemon laws that cover used vehicles are in effect in Connecticut, the District of Columbia, Massachusetts, Minnesota, New York, and Rhode Island. Each law varies as to the age of the vehicle, its mileage, and cost. The Massachusetts law requires mandatory but limited warranty protection on used vehicles for engines, transmissions, steering mechanisms, and brakes. For used vehicles with less than 40,000 miles at the time of purchase, the warranty period is 90 days or 3,750 miles; vehicles with between 40,000 and 79,999 miles must be warranted for 60 days or 1000 miles; for those with between 80,000 and 124,999, the warranty must be for 30 days or 750 miles. Before a consumer can get a refund, the dealer must be given three repair attempts for the same defect or the car must be out of service for 11 business days. Massachusetts also requires auto dealers to give a consumer a refund should the vehicle fail state safety inspection within 7 days of purchase and if the inspection-related repairs are expected to cost more than 10 percent of the purchase price.

Used Vehicle Lemon Branding Laws

About 34 states require that vehicles that have to be repurchased by a seller under a state lemon law requirement (a vehicle with serious defects) must then be labeled to describe that fact. The law specifies that the title of a vehicle be properly branded with a clear indication that the vehicle was a lemon and that disclosure must be made to consumers at the point of sale.

Vehicle Repair Laws

Most states have a Vehicle Repair Law designed to protect consumers from unscrupulous merchants because this is typically the number one complaint of consumers to government agencies. Unfair and deceptive practices abound in the auto repair industry.

Generally, such laws provides that on request, a consumer must be given a written repair estimate from someone that is going to repair his or her vehicle, unless the business is unwilling to do the repair. Later, if the mechanic or body repair person determines that the repairs are going to cost more than 10 percent above the estimate, the shop must obtain the consumer's permission to go ahead at the higher price. No charges are allowed for unauthorized work.

It is also illegal for repair shops to suggest that certain repairs are necessary or desirable when such is not the case. Finally, a consumer has the right to get back any parts replaced by the repair shop. If covered by a warranty or rebuilding arrangement, the consumer may view the parts, but may not be able to keep them.

Secret Warranty Disclosure Laws for Automobiles

For many years, automobile manufacturers have offer **secret automobile warranties** that provided free repairs or reimbursement of incurred expenses when persistent problems develop beyond the traditional warranty time period. The problems usually affect the vehicle's performance or safety, but are not the subject of a formal recall. Secret warranties offered by auto manufacturers are disclosed in **factory service bulletins** that are sent to dealers authorizing them to make the repairs. In such cases, the dealers, not consumers, are notified. Historically, the dealers have been allowed to offer to make repairs at their discretion, and only those owners who complain the loudest received the free repairs. About 500 secret automobile warranties are in effect at any point in time. Manufacturers sometimes call these efforts **policy adjustments** or **good-will service**. What is especially bad about secret auto warranties is that not all affected consumers benefit since most owners remain unaware of the manufacturer's policies.

Only a few states (CA, CN, VA, and WS) have secret warranty disclosure laws for automobiles that require the manufacturers and dealers to notify all affected owners when such repairs will be paid for by the manufacturer. These laws typically require auto manufacturers to notify by first-class mail all owners that may be afected by a manufacturer's warranty adjustment program . This includes notifying those owners who have already paid for the relevant repairs; therefore, those consumers may obtain reimbursement. Dealers also must tell consumers who have purchased an extended warranty if a particular repair is covered under such a program; dealers also must tell consumers if future repairs could be covered under an extended warranty. In some states, consumers are allowed to sue and collect damages from any auto manufacturer who violates the secret warranty disclosure law.

Federal Trade Commission Used Car Rule[1]

Each year, Americans spend about $100 billion to buy more than 17 million used cars. If you are buying a used car, the Federal Trade Commission's Used Car Rule may help you.

The rule requires all used car dealers to place a large sticker, called a *buyer's guide*, in the window of each used vehicle they offer for sale. The buyer's guide will state:

- Whether the vehicle comes with a warranty, and if so, what specific warranty protection the dealer will provide.
- Whether the vehicle comes with no warranty ("as is") or with implied warranties only.
- That you should ask to have the car inspected by your own mechanic before you buy.
- That you should get all promises in writing.
- What some of the major problems are that may occur in any car.

---

[1]Source: Buying a used car (1985, May). *Facts for consumers*. Federal Trade Commission, Bureau of Consumer Protection, Office of Consumer/Business Education, Washington, D.C.

Whenever you purchase a used car from a dealer, you should receive the original or an identical copy of the buyer's guide that appeared in the window of the vehicle you bought. The buyer's guide must reflect any changes in warranty coverage that you may have negotiated with the dealer. It also becomes a part of your sales contract and overrides any contrary provisions that may be in that contract.

Dealers are required to post the buyer's guide on all used vehicles, including used automobiles, light-duty vans, and light-duty trucks. A **used vehicle** is one that has been driven more than the distance necessary to deliver a new car to the dealership or to test drive it. Therefore, "demonstrator" cars are covered by the rule. Motorcycles are excluded.

Warranty Information in the Buyer's Guide

A major portion of the buyer's guide gives you new and important information you can use when you select a used car. In the past, lack of information and misunderstanding about warranties frequently were a source of consumer problems. The following section explains the warranty portion of the buyer's guide. The buyer's guide is shown so that you can understand the information that follows.

A. "As is"

About one-half of all used cars sold by dealers come without a warranty, or "**as is**." This means that if you have problems with the car after you buy it, you must pay for any needed repairs yourself. The dealer has no further responsibility for the car once the sale is complete and you drive off the lot. If the dealer offers a vehicle for sale "as is", without any warranties, the box provided next to the "as is" disclosure will be checked.

B. Implied Warranties Only

Under most state laws, almost every purchase you make from a merchant is covered by an implied warranty, unless the seller tells you in writing that implied warranties do not apply. The most common type of implied warranty is called a **warranty of merchantability**. This means that the seller promises that the product will do what it is supposed to do. For example, a car will run; a toaster will toast.

Another type of implied warranty is the **warranty of fitness for a particular purpose**. This applies when you buy a vehicle on the dealer's advice that it is suitable for a particular use. For example, a dealer who suggests that you buy a specific vehicle for hauling a trailer warrants, in effect, that the vehicle will be suitable for hauling a trailer.

If your vehicle does not come with a written warranty, it is still covered by implied warranties unless the buyer's guide is marked "as is". Several states (Kansas, Maine, Maryland, Massachusetts, Mississippi, New York, Vermont, West Virginia, and the District of Columbia) do not permit "as is" sales. In these states, dealers must sell their vehicles with implied warranties.

If problems arise that are not covered by the written warranty, you should investigate the protection given by implied warranties. Implied warranty coverage varies from state to state. Your state consumer protection office may be able to provide more information about specific implied warranty coverage in your state.

In those states that do not permit "as is" sales by dealers, or if the dealer offers a vehicle with only implied warranties, a disclosure entitled "Implied Warranties Only" will be printed on the buyer's guide in place of the "As Is" disclosure. The box next to this disclosure would be checked if the dealer chooses to sell the car with implied warranties and no written warranty. A copy of the "Implied Warranties Only" disclosure is shown below.

C. Warranties

If dealers offer a warranty on a used vehicle, they must fill in the warranty portion of the buyer's guide. Examine the warranty carefully *before* you buy to see what is covered and what is not. The warranty that the dealer offers may give you some idea of what the dealer thinks about the condition of the vehicle.

If the dealer makes any promises to repair the vehicle that are not listed on the buyer's guide, ask the dealer to add those promises to both the buyer's guide and the sales contract. The sales contract also must include other specific information about your warranty.

Look for the Following Information on the Buyer's Guide

D. See if the warranty offered is "full" or "limited." A **full warranty** provides the following terms and conditions:

- Warranty service will be provided to anyone who owns the vehicle during the warranty period when a problem is reported. Warranty service will be provided free of charge, including such costs as returning the vehicle or removing and reinstalling a system covered by the warranty, when necessary.
- At your choice, the dealer will provide either a replacement or a full refund if the dealer is unable, after a reasonable number of tries, to repair the vehicle or a system covered by the warranty.
- Warranty service is provided without requiring that you return a warranty registration card.
- No limit is placed on the duration of implied warranties.

If any one of the preceding statements is not true, then the warranty is limited. A full or limited warranty need not cover the entire vehicle. The dealer may specify only certain systems for coverage under a warranty. By giving a **limited warranty**, the dealer is telling you that there are some costs or responsibilities that the dealer will not assume for systems covered by the warranty.

E. Check the percentage of the repair cost that the dealer will pay. For example, "the dealer will pay 100% of the labor and 100% of the parts..."

F. Check which specific systems are covered. The exact systems (such as frame and body, brake system, etc.) covered must be listed. A list of descriptive names for the major systems of an automobile is printed on the back of the buyer's guide.

G. Check the duration of the warranty for each covered system. For example, "30 days or 1000 miles, whichever occurs first."

Unexpired Manufacturer's Warranties

If the used vehicle is still covered under the terms of the manufacturer's original warranty, the dealer may add the following paragraph in the space below the warranty disclosure.

> MANUFACTURER'S WARRANTY STILL APPLIES. The manufacturer's original warranty has not expired on the vehicle. Consult the manufacturer's warranty booklet for details as to warranty coverage, service location, etc. This does not necessarily mean that dealers also offer *their own* warranty in addition to the manufacturer's. If you have any questions about warranty coverage, ask the dealer to let you examine any unexpired warranty on the vehicle.

Other Sections of the Buyer's Guide

There are other important parts of the buyer's guide. These parts are explained below and are also noted on the sample buyer's guide in Figure 11-1.

H. Spoken Promises

A statement appears on the buyer's guide that warns consumers not to rely on spoken promises. Oral promises are difficult, if not impossible, to enforce. Have the dealership put any promises in writing, or do not count on the promise.

This statement also reminds you to keep the buyer's guide after purchasing the vehicle. The buyer's guide will serve as proof of written promises.

I. Service Contracts

When you buy a car, you may be offered a **service contract**. Although often called **extended warranties**, service contracts are not warranties. Warranties are included in the price of the product. Service contracts come separately from the vehicle, at an extra cost. To decide whether you need a service contract, you should consider several factors: whether the warranty already covers the repairs that you would get under the service contract, whether the vehicle is likely to need repairs and their potential costs, how long the service contract is in effect, and the reputation of the dealer offering the service contract.

If a service contract is offered, the dealer will mark the box provided. However, in those states which regulate service contracts under their insurance laws, the dealer is not required to include this disclosure on the buyer's guide. Therefore, if you do not see the disclosure, ask the salesperson about the availability of a service contract.

Remember, when you purchase a service contract within 90 days of buying the vehicle, federal law prohibits the dealer from disclaiming implied warranties on the systems covered in that service contract. For example, if you buy a car "as is", the car normally will not be covered by implied warranties. But if you also buy a service contract covering the engine for 6 months, you automatically get implied warranties on the engine as well, which may give you additional protection even beyond the scope of the service contract.

Chapter 11: Laws on Vehicles 125

BUYER'S GUIDE

H IMPORTANT: Spoken promises are difficult to enforce. Ask the dealer to put all promises in writing. Keep this form.

VEHICLE MAKE   MODEL   YEAR   VIN NUMBER

DEALER STOCK NUMBER (Optional)

WARRANTIES FOR THIS VEHICLE:

A

☐ **AS IS - NO WARRANTY**

YOU WILL PAY ALL COSTS FOR ANY REPAIRS. The dealer assumes no responsibility for any repairs regardless of any oral statements about the vehicle.

C

☐ **WARRANTY**

E

☐ FULL ☐ LIMITED WARRANTY: The dealer will pay _____% of the labor and _____% of the parts for the covered systems that fail during the warranty period. Ask the dealer for a copy of the warranty document for a full explanation of warranty coverage, exclusions, and the dealer's repair obligations. Under state law, "implied warranties" may give you even more rights.

D

SYSTEMS COVERED: DURATION:

_____   _____
_____   _____
_____   _____
_____**F**_____   _____**G**_____
_____   _____
_____   _____
_____   _____

I ☐ SERVICE CONTRACT. A service contract is available at an extra charge on this vehicle. Ask for details as to coverage, deductible, price, and exclusions. If you buy a service contract within 90 days of the time of sale, state law "implied warranties" may give you additional rights.

J PRE PURCHASE INSPECTION: ASK THE DEALER IF YOU MAY HAVE THIS VEHICLE INSPECTED BY YOUR MECHANIC EITHER ON OR OFF THE LOT.

SEE THE BACK OF THIS FORM for important additional information, including a list of some major defects that may occur in used motor vehicles.

B

☐ **IMPLIED WARRANTIES ONLY**

This means that the dealer does not make any specific promises to fix things that need repair when you buy the vehicle or after the time of sale. But, state law "implied warranties" may give you some rights to have the dealer take care of serious problems that were not apparent when you bought the vehicle.

FIGURE 11-1 A Typical Buyer's Guide

Below is a list of some major defects that may occur in used motor vehicles.

Frame & Body
   Frame-cracks, corrective welds, or rusted through
   Dogtracks—bent or twisted frame

Engine
   Oil leakage, excluding normal seepage
   Cracked block or head
   Belts missing or inoperable
   Knocks or misses related to camshaft lifters and push rods
   Abnormal exhaust discharge

Transmission & Drive Shaft
   Improper fluid level or leakage, excluding normal seepage
   Cracked or damaged case which is visible
   Abnormal noise or vibration caused by faulty transmission or drive shaft
   Improper shifting or functioning in any gear
   Manual clutch slips or chatters

Differential
   Improper fluid level or leakage excluding normal seepage
   Cracked or damaged housing which is visible
   Abnormal noise or vibration caused by faulty differential

Cooling System
   Leakage including radiator
   Improperly functioning water pump

Electrical System
   Battery leakage
   Improperly functioning alternator, generator, battery, or starter

Fuel System
   Visible leakage

Inoperable Accessories
   Gauges or warning devices
   Air conditioner
   Heater & Defroster

Brake System
   Failure warning light broken
   Pedal not firm under pressure (DOT spec.)
   Not enough pedal reserve (DOT spec.)
   Does not stop vehicle in straight line (DOT spec.)
   Hoses damaged
   Drum or rotor too thin (Mfgr. Specs)
   Lining or pad thickness less than 1/32 inch
   Power unit not operating or leaking
   Structural or mechanical parts damaged

Steering System
   Too much free play at steering wheel (DOT specs.)
   Free play in linkage more than 1/4 inch
   Steering gear binds or jams
   Front wheels aligned improperly (DOT specs.)
   Power unit belts cracked or slipping
   Power unit fluid level improper

Suspension System
   Ball joint seals damaged
   Structural parts bent or damaged
   Stabilizer bar disconnected
   Spring broken
   Shock absorber mounting loose
   Rubber bushings damaged or missing
   Radius rod damaged or missing
   Shock absorber leaking or functioning improperly

Tires
   Tread depth less than 2/32 inch
   Sizes mismatched
   Visible damage

Wheels
   Visible cracks, damage or repairs
   Mounting bolts loose or missing

Exhaust System
   Leakage

DEALER

ADDRESS

SEE FOR COMPLAINTS

FIGURE 11-1 (continued) A Typical Buyer's Guide

Chapter 11: *Laws on Vehicles* 127

J. Prepurchase Independent Inspection

The buyer's guide also includes a suggestion that you ask the dealer whether you may have the vehicle inspected by your own mechanic either on or off the premises. An independent inspection lets you find out about the mechanical condition of the vehicle *before* you buy it.

Some dealers will permit you to take the car to an independent mechanic. Others may have good reasons (for example, insurance restrictions) for denying this request.

With the dealer's permission, you can bring an independent mechanic to the used car lot. If you do not already have a mechanic you rely on, ask someone who knows about cars for the names of competent, reputable mechanics. You also can find mechanics through advertisements, car repair establishments, automobile associations, and automobile diagnostic centers in your community.

K. Vehicle Systems

The buyer's guide includes a list of the 14 major systems of an automobile and some of the major problems that may occur in these systems. You may find this list helpful to evaluate the mechanical condition of the vehicle. The list also may be useful when comparing warranties offered on different cars or by different dealers.

L. Dealer Identification and Consumer Complaint Information

On the back of the buyer's guide you will find the name and address of the dealership. In the space below that you will find the name and telephone number of the person at the dealership who should be contacted if any complaints arise after the sale.

Additional Information

Private Sales

If you buy a used car from a private individual (for example, through a classified newspaper ad), the sale is not covered by the rule. Private sellers do not have to use the buyer's guide. In most private sales, the car is sold "as is". Without a written contract with specific repair provisions, the private seller in most states has no further responsibility for the car. If you have a written contract, the seller must live up to the promises stated in the contract. Depending on its age, the car may be covered by a manufacturer's warranty or service contract. Ask the seller to let you examine any unexpired warranty or service contract on the vehicle.

Even without the buyer's guide, when you buy a used vehicle from a private party, you can follow the suggestions given here. For example, refer to the list of potential problems in the buyer's guide. In addition, ask the seller whether you may have the vehicle inspected by your own mechanic. It is important to find out about the mechanical condition of the vehicle before you buy it.

Spanish-Language Sales

If you buy a used car and the sales talk is conducted in Spanish, you are entitled to see and keep a Spanish-language version of the buyer's guide. The Used Car Rule includes a text for the Spanish-language version.

Chapter 12

Laws on Warranties

State laws throughout the country offer strong warranty protections for consumers. State laws cover both express and implied warranties, and they generally offer stronger warranty protections than federal law. This was examined in Chapter 7. This chapter overviews the additional consumer information and protections provided in the federal Magnuson-Moss Warranty Act.

Magnuson-Moss Warranty Act

The conflicting viewpoints of consumers and sellers has historically resulted in warranty problems. The concept of warranties that used to give consumers dissatisfaction because of a lack of clarity and deceptions perhaps can best be summed up by the old adage, "The bold print giveth and the fine print taketh away." As a result, governments have written laws to govern warranty situations. The Magnuson-Moss Warranty Act was passed in 1975. It authorized the Federal Trade Commission to write regulations that interpret and implement the law, primarily through an effort to require disclosure of warranty terms. The Magnuson-Moss Warranty Act attempts to restore a sense of fair play in the marketplace by giving consumers an understanding of warranties more equal to that of the sellers.

A **warranty** or (**guarantee**) is an assurance by a seller that the goods or property sold are of the quality represented or will be as promised. Warranties on consumer products are offered by manufacturers as a promotional device to help differentiate one product from its competitors. In fact, whole advertising campaigns are sometimes designed around a product warranty.

The seller sees the warranty as something that limits the firm's liability, since it legally obligates the manufacturer only so far in dealing with buyers who have problems while simultaneously inducing particular expectations on the part of the consumer. For example, a written warranty may specify which remedies are available to consumers with problems and may limit how much the company will pay. An **express warranty** is a written guarantee setting out specific assurances by the manufacturer or seller.

The consumer, however, views warranties in a different light. Many consumers accept warranties uncritically, assuming that the act of offering a warranty suggests that this is a quality product.

Standards for Companies that Offer Warranties

The Magnuson-Moss law and subsequent regulations do not require that a manufacturer offer a guarantee, but if a manufacturer does offer a written warranty, it must comply with various standards. Basically the law demands that a warranty should mean what it says and that the details should be spelled out in easy-to-understand language. Therefore, products claiming a "money-back guarantee", suggesting that they are "fully guaranteed", or promising "satisfaction guaranteed or your money back", should do what is promised. Sellers are prohibited from giving something to consumers with the big print and taking it away with the small print.

Warranties must use clear and simple language to tell the following: (1) the name and address of the warrantor, (2) whether the warranty is given only to the original purchaser, (3) a description of exactly what is warranted and for how long, (4) an indication that a registration card must be returned if that is the warrantor's procedure, (5) the procedure for placing a claim, (6) what the company will do in case of problems, and (7) step-by-step procedures to follow to settle a dispute between the buyer and the seller.

To reduce problems with warranties, the Magnuson-Moss law requires that consumers be able to examine warranty coverage before they make a purchase. Any product that costs $15 or more is covered under the law and must be made available for inspection. Either sellers can print the warranty on the outside of the product package or retailers must post a sign near products that have warranties indicating where in the store a customer can go to examine the warranty.

Disclaiming Implied Warranties is Prohibited

The law has improved the opportunity for consumers to understand and practice their warranty rights. However, there are still definite problems of comprehension because it is doubtful that many consumers can understand such legal concepts as "incidental and consequential damages" and disclaimers such as "the above limitation or exclusion may not apply to you." Further, written warranties typically take paragraph after paragraph to state the limitations of the seller and what is not covered. Note however, that the Magnuson-Moss law prohibits warrantors from disclaiming implied warranties and it requires that they include sentences in written warranties that tell buyers that they *may* have certain rights according to state laws.

To illustrate, the implied warranty rights of merchantability and fitness for a particular purpose provided under state law are protected by the Magnuson-Moss Warranty Act. This is why written warranties typically end with a sentence saying, "This warranty gives you specific legal rights, and you may also have other rights which vary from state to state."

Another problem exists with the lack of uniformity of state laws limiting liability for incidental and consequential damages. For example, your warranted antifreeze may not perform as advertised, leading to a frozen engine needing $2000 in consequential repairs. There also could be incidental towing costs to get the vehicle to the repair shop. The Magnuson-Moss Warranty Act simply requires that written guarantees clearly say that, "Some states do not allow limitations of incidental or consequential damages, so the above limitations may not apply to you." Thus, consumers still may have incidental and consequential implied warranty rights in the states where they live.

States vary as to how long implied warranty rights last. Magnuson-Moss requires that warranties include the statement that, "Some states do not allow limitations on how long an implied warranty lasts, so the above limitations may not apply to you." Although these phrases are accurate and provide important protection for consumers, they seem to confuse rather than clarify the issues. To secure these rights under the Uniform Commercial Code of state laws, consumers have to resort to civil lawsuits.

Full and Limited Warranties May Be Offered

The law requires that express guarantees be conspicuously designated as either full or limited, which immediately gives consumers an indication of the type of warranty coverage provided. To meet the federal standards to be a **full warranty**, the warrantor must: (1) remedy a defective product within a reasonable time and without charge in the event of a defect, malfunction, or failure to conform to the warranty, and (2) after a reasonable number of attempts by the warrantor to remedy defects, the warrantor must give the consumer the option of either a refund or replacement without charge. The latter part of this definition is known as a **lemon clause** because it provides recourse to buyers who are stuck with products that seem to be unrepairable. Replacements must be made free of charge, including removal and reinstallation, while warrantors may deduct an amount for depreciation based on actual use when they replace products. In addition, another requirement for full warranties is that the consumer must not have to do anything unreasonable to get warranty service, such as return a heavy product, like a washing machine, to the seller. Full warranties cannot require the return of a warranty registration card either.

The FTC has the authority to define what is a reasonable number of repairs for various products. Consumers with persistent automobile complaints can use the power of lemon clauses for cars with full warranties, as well as state lemon laws to motivate sellers to make proper repairs. It is also important to note that products offering full warranties cannot place limits on the duration of implied warranties; thus a warrantor offering a full warranty is liable for any incidental and consequential damages, such as food, lodging, towing, car rental fees, and food spoilage. Full warranties apply to both the original purchaser and subsequent owners during the Warranty period.

Limited Warranties are much more widespread because of the severe obligations placed on sellers offering full warranties. A **limited warranty** is any written guarantee that provides less than a full warranty. If any full warranty requirement is not provided in a warranty, the warranty is classified as a limited warranty. For example, a limited warranty may cover parts only, instead of parts and labor, or it may cover repairs only, instead of replacement or refund. Many limited warranties require that the buyer has to return a warranty card to activate the warranty. Nevertheless, many limited warranties provide excellent coverage on consumer products.

Informal Dispute Procedures Are Encouraged

The Magnuson-Moss Warranty Act encourages the use of an **informal dispute procedure** whenever warranty problems arise between sellers and buyers. Such a procedure allows impartial people to review the arguments and evidence of the complaining consumer and the seller in an attempt to resolve the conflict about warranty service. Warrantors are not required to set up such procedures, but when they do, the procedures must meet minimum standards established by the FTC (known as Rule 703) and explain the details in their written warranties. When a warrantor has established an informal dispute procedure, the consumer must use it before taking any legal action. Therefore, manufacturers are motivated to set up an informal dispute procedure as an alternative to engaging in costly litigation with consumers with warranty service problems. Rule 703 requires that consumer disputes be settled within a 40-day time period.

Consumers who successfully file state or federal lawsuits against warrantors who do not have an informal dispute procedure may be awarded their purchase costs, attorneys fees, and damages. In addition, consumers injured by a breach of warranty may file a federal class action lawsuit. Few warranty problems meet all the restrictions necessary for consumers to economically and successfully pursue a class action lawsuit under the provisions of the Magnuson-Moss Warranty Act.

The Magnuson-Moss Warranty Act does not preempt the field of state warranty law. Instead, it adds another layer of consumer protection while preserving rights and remedies under state law.

Chapter 13

Laws on Housing

Housing is an area of consumer spending vital to the consumer interest. The need for suitable housing is a challenge that all consumers face, yet often the supply and quality of housing is not the best. Renters especially need to know their tenant rights to be able to enforce them. People's housing problems are compounded when faced with discrimination.

Laws and Regulations on Housing

A number of laws and regulations that exist in the area of housing are described below, including: (1) Renter's Security Deposits, (2) Late Possession of the Rental Property (3) Habitability of Rental Unit, (4) Tenants Making Minor Repairs, (5) Community Reinvestment Act, (6) Fair Housing Act, (7) Home Mortgage Disclosure Act, and (8) State Housing Discrimination Laws.

Renter's Security Deposits

Almost all states have laws governing security deposits paid by renters to landlords. Typically, a landlord cannot collect more than one month's rent as a security deposit. That amount must be held in an interest-bearing bank account, and the interest must be paid to the tenant within 30 days of the yearly anniversary date of tenancy. At the end of the tenancy, the landlord may only deduct for unpaid rent and for damages beyond reasonable wear and tear. Security deposits must be returned, noting deductions, within 30 days after the tenancy ends, otherwise the consumer may be entitled to double or triple damages.

Late Possession of the Rental Property

Sometimes consumers experience difficulty in taking possession of rental housing because the landlord cannot deliver the unit. The problem may be that the previous tenant will not move out, or the landlord may find that it will take more time to put the facility into proper condition. Regardless of the reason, this may cost the renter extra money in the form of motel expenses until the move can be made.

In all states, consumers so wronged have the right to sue in an attempt to collect damages from the landlord. He or she should be forced to reimburse the renter for costs of lodging elsewhere, plus any storage expenses. It is easy to win such lawsuits where there is a "damages" clause in the lease contract; such lawsuits will fail if the lease contains a clause that totally absolves the landlord of any liability in such situations. In such cases, the dispute may be resolved by compromises made between the landlord and the tenant.

Habitability of Rental Unit

All states and municipalities provide legal rights to tenants. The habitability of the rental unit must meet some legally prescribed minimum standard, such as running water, functional toilets, heat during the months of fall, winter and spring, and a working stove. In most states, an implied warranty covers the availability of heat and the safety of access areas, such as stairs. Filing a lawsuit against a landlord for nonperformance is permitted in all states. This is usually done in a small claims court (described in Chapter 8), where for a nominal filing fee (perhaps $15) lawsuits up to a certain dollar amount (perhaps $2500) can be pursued without an attorney.

In addition, reporting building-code violations to a local government housing authority is not just cause for eviction or for harassment in the form of a rent increase or utility shutoff. Also, joining a tenant organization is not cause for eviction; tenant organizations aim to improve the bargaining power of tenants.

Tenants Sometimes May Make Minor Repairs

In many states, tenants may legally make minor repairs themselves and deduct those costs from their next rent payment. This is subject to certain restrictions, such as giving sufficient prior written notification to the landlord.

Interstate Land Sales

The Interstate Land Sales Full Disclosure Act (passed in 1968) is designed to help consumers avoid land sale scams. The law requires developers who are selling (or leasing) 100 or more unimproved lots across state lines to file detailed information about their properties with the Department of Housing and Urban Development. Before signing a contract, the developer is required to show consumers the **property report**, which describes relevant details about the venture. In addition, consumers have a seven-day cooling off period during which they may change their minds (for misrepresentation or any other reason). When considering buying undeveloped land that is exempt from this law, people are advised to be certain that the contract includes a cancellation clause.

Community Reinvestment Act

The Community Reinvestment Act (CRA) requires federal agencies to encourage depository financial institutions to help meet the credit needs of their communities, especially low- and moderate-income neighborhoods. The federal regulatory agencies, such as the Federal Reserve Board, assess the institutions' records of meeting those credit needs by preparing a written evaluation of the institutions along with the assignment of a concluding rating supported with facts. These are disclosed to the public. Lenders must tell inquiring consumers their CRA rating.

Fair Housing Act

Discrimination is acting on the basis of bias or intentional prejudice. It is illegal to discriminate in the financing of housing. Various laws prohibit discrimination on the basis of race, color, religion, national origin, sex, elderliness, parenthood, or handicap.

The Fair Housing Act prohibits discrimination on the basis of race, color, sex, religion, handicap, familial status, or national origin in the financing, sale, or rental of housing. The Fair Housing Act directly prohibits discrimination in mortgage lending. It empowers the Department of Housing and Urban Development and the Attorney General

> **CONSUMER UPDATE:**
> **Community Reinvestment Act Ratings**
>
> Because of the Community Reinvestment Act (CRA), as amended in 1990, banks, savings banks, and savings and loan associations are required to serve the convenience and needs of the communities where they have offices, especially low- and moderate-income neighborhoods. The CRA regulations, described in Chapter 5, require a dialogue between the financial institutions and all segments of the communities they serve.
>
> The CRA requires that financial institutions play a vital role in revitalizing neighborhoods. The accountability of the banks, savings banks, and savings and loan associations is made clear to the public through posting of regular performance evaluations, **CRA ratings**, that are used to grade each institution's efforts to serve its community. This rating is based upon proper documentation reviewed by federal inspectors. Interested consumers need only visit a local financial institution to determine its CRA rating and review the institution's CRA Public File for a description of recent efforts.

to help assure non-discriminatory practices in all aspects of the housing market. For example, it is illegal to discriminate against families with children when renting or selling a house or apartment. The Justice Department can ask for compensatory monetary damages for persons victimized and assess civil penalties. The maximum civil penalty for a first finding of discrimination is $50,000, and up to $100,000 for a subsequent violation.

Home Mortgage Disclosure Act

The Home Mortgage Disclosure Act (HMDA) requires certain lending institutions to report annually on their mortgage lending practices, including both originations and purchases of home purchases and home improvement loans, as well as applications for such loans. The type of loan, location of the property, race or national origin, gender, and income of the applicant are reported. Such information, which aggregately must be disclosed to the public, can help determine how well institutions are serving the housing credit needs of neighborhoods and communities. Lenders must post a notice of lending availability in their public lobby.

These data also allow others to check on any discrimination in the pattern of lending. Recent data from the Federal Reserve Board reveal that while 11 percent of white people are rejected for home loans, the figure is 24 percent for blacks. These numbers do not prove that discrimination is occurring in housing lending, but they do suggest that discrimination may be happening. Consumers need to be aware of the housing laws that can be used to protect them.

State Housing Discrimination Laws

In addition to the federal regulations prohibiting discrimination, all states have fair housing laws with similar purposes. The typical state law protects against the following acts: (1) refusal to sell or rent or to deal or negotiate with any person, (2) presenting

Chapter 13: *Laws on Housing* 137

CONSUMER UPDATE
How to Identify Discrimination—Some Examples

To help combat discrimination, the Clinton Administration directed that all federal agencies meet and develop a uniform "Policy Statement on Discrimination in Lending" for detecting and preventing the many forms subtle discrimination can take. The policy newly's approved statement applies to all lenders, including mortgage brokers, issuers of credit cards, and any other person who extends credit of any type. The agencies define **discrimination in lending** as lending on the basis of race or other prohibited factors and that such discrimination is destructive, morally repugnant, and against the law.

The agencies also offered a series of examples of discrimination, some of which are summarized below:

- A lender rejected a loan application made by a female applicant with flaws in her credit report but accepted applications by male applicants with similar flaws.
- Two minority applicants were told that it would take several hours and require the payment of an application fee to determine whether or not they qualified for a home loan, while non-minority applicants were given no such requirements.
- When a non-minority couple applied for a loan, upon questioning the lender recommended that the adverse information in their credit report be challenged because it was incorrect and the loan was later approved. A minority couple with similar adverse information was simply denied credit without having an opportunity to discuss the report.
- Two minority borrowers inquired about a mortgage loan and were given applications for fixed-rate loans only and were not offered assistance in completing the applications; later their application was turned down. Two similarly qualified non-minority applicants made an identical inquiry, were given information about adjustable-rate and fixed rate loans and were given assistance in filling out the application which the lender later approved.
- A lender's longtime policy has been not to extend loans for single family residences for less than $60,000. However, this policy is shown to disproportionately exclude potential minority applicants.

CONSUMER UPDATE:
Help for Low-Income Home Buyers

A number of housing loan programs exist for low-income consumers. Key among them is the Federal National Mortgage Association (Fannie Mae). Its newest program allows borrowers to make a down payment of as little as $1000, or three percent of the sales price. Participant's income is not to exceed 60 to 80 percent of the area's median income. The Washington, D.C. area has the highest median income in the program, over $59,000.

All states have funds reserved to subsidize interest rates for low-income home buyers. For example, if housing loans are 8 percent and require a $440 monthly repayment amount for a $60,000 loan, a government subsidy could reduce the interest rate perhaps to 6 percent. Then the monthly payment for principal and interest would be $359, perhaps more affordable than $440. The maximum income ceiling for participation may be about $29,000 for a single and $35,000 for a couple. A great number of housing loan programs are community based and can only be learned about by contacting local housing officials. If interested, see the telephone book blue pages to find out about income requirements and other details.

different terms and conditions to different people for buying or renting housing, (3) advertising that housing is available to certain persons, (4) denying housing is available for inspection, sale, or rent when it really is available, (5) **blockbusting**, which is persuasion of owners to sell or rent housing by telling them that priority groups are moving into the neighborhood, (6) denying or making different conditions or terms for home loans by commercial lenders, and (7) **redlining,** which is drawing a red line (or any other color for that matter) around areas of a community and refusing loans to people wanting financing in those areas.

DID YOU KNOW?
How to Report Discrimination
If you suspect that you have been discriminated against because of your race, gender, or age, telephone any of the following: Housing Discrimination Hotline of the Department of Housing and Urban Development (800-669-9777); Justice Department (202-514-4713); National Fair Housing Alliance (202-898-1661).

A number of exclusions to federal and state laws usually exist. An exclusion usually occurs when a private individual sells or rents a home without employing a real estate broker, without using discriminatory advertising, and without having sold more than one residence in the past 2 years. The laws also are not applicable to the rental of rooms or units in buildings of not more than four families if the owner lives in one of the units and if no discriminatory advertising is used. Also, religious organizations or private clubs may give preferences to their members in housing.

Chapter 14

Sample Complaint Letters

This chapter includes suggestions on how to write a letter of complaint. Six sample complaint letters are illustrated. The first is a general complaint letter. The next four have to do with complaining to dispute an item on a credit card bill. The last letter provides an example of a "consumer statement" to add to one's credit report to tell his/her side of a dispute. All these letters help consumers assert their rights in various marketplace transactions.

How to Write a Letter of Complaint

Don't put up with poor treatment by sellers or government agencies. Do not accept being "brushed off" by someone in authority. If you cannot think clearly when someone is pressuring you, go away and take some time to think. Then sit down and make some notes of things to say. Either go back later and complain or write a letter of complaint.

When writing a consumer complaint letter, type the letter on business-size paper and aim your communication at the right person. Sometimes it's the consumer affairs office, sometimes it's the company president or chief executive officer (CEO). A reference section librarian can locate corporate names and addresses. The "Who's Who" books have the home addresses of lots of big name executives.

1. Explain the problem. Be clear and concise in explaining the problem. Be factual, and do not dwell on sensitive issues. Avoid being sarcastic or overly emotional; let them know that you are a reasonable person. Try to say it all in one sentence, and add clarifying statements if needed. Also, tell the story of what you have already done in attempting to resolve the problem.

2. Identify your expectations. Be firm and courteous when requesting (don't demand) what it is that you want the seller to do. Do you want something repaired, a product replaced, or a refund? Give choices, if appropriate.

3. Give persuasive reasons. Sellers are people just like everyone else, and they like to be treated with both intelligence and respect. Give logical reasons why the action you want is, first, the right thing to do and, second, also in the best interest of the seller. If you have been a long-time customer, tell the seller, especially if you intend to buy from that seller in the future.

4. Document your request. No seller is going to do what you want without a little proof, so include appropriate documentation. Sellers want to see such things as a receipt for proof of purchase, a canceled check, a charge slip, or a service invoice. Never send originals because they may become lost. If such documentation is no longer available, just explain why.

5. Use an action close. The way to get action is to ask for it. Therefore, in a positive way, tell what action you will take next should the seller not respond affirmatively within an appropriate time period. Give a reasonable deadline. Include your address and telephone number.

A second complaint letter (and, if necessary, the third, fourth, and fifth) should briefly repeat the problem, remind them that they have not yet responded to your letter (or the response was unsatisfactory), and tell them you will now complain to third-party agencies. Also, enclose photocopies of any previous correspondence.

SAMPLE COMPLAINT LETTER TO MERCHANT OR MANUFACTURER

Your address
Your city, state, and ZIP code
Today's date

Name of person (if known)
Job title
Company name
Street address
City, state, and zip code

Dear Reader (use correct name if known):

I am writing to tell you of my dissatisfaction with (name of product and its serial number or the service performed), which was purchased (tell where and when). The exact problem is that the product (tell the reasons for the complaint, that it no longer functions, is wrong for the task, or whatever). What I have already done to try and resolve the problem is (tell the story of what occurred as well as the actions and statements of particular salespersons or managers).

In order to resolve this problem, I think that you should (state what specific action or actions you believe the seller should take on your behalf).

In all fairness, your company should (give the refund, exchange the product, or whatever) for the following reasons. (Give two or more reasons whenever possible).

Enclosed are photocopies of (sales receipt, invoice, previous letters, whatever) that support my request for action. Please note (in one specific document) that (focus the reader's attention on a particular item you want them to be sure and see because it supports your position).

I look forward to receiving your reply providing a speedy resolution to this problem, and I will allow three weeks before referring it to the appropriate government consumer protection agency. Please write to me at the above address or contact me by telephone (give both home and work numbers if it would otherwise be difficult to locate you during daytime hours).

Sincerely,

Your name

Enclosures (include copies of appropriate documents)

**COMPLAINT LETTER
TO DISPUTE AN ITEM ON A CREDIT CARD BILL**
(For an error, an unauthorized charge, or dissatisfaction with the goods or services)

Return address
Today's date

Name and address of credit card issuer

Dear reader (use correct name if known):

RE: Credit Card Charge Account #(put your number here)

I am writing today to complain about a charge that appeared on my recent bill. The amount of (give dollar figure here) that appeared on my bill with a date of (give date here) is in error.

The reason why the amount on my bill is being challenged is that (an error, an unauthorized charge, or dissatisfaction with the goods or services). (Explain your side of the situation more fully. If appropriate, explain why you are willing to accept a partial credit rather than a full credit.)

Therefore, I expect that (name of credit card company) will immediately credit my account for the challenged amount (and, if appropriate, remove any interest assessed on that particular charge). (If appropriate, also say that you assume that the credit card company will reinvestigate this transaction and send you a letter reporting the findings.) I fully expect that my credit card account with (name of credit card company) will remain credited in the amount of (put amount here).

Thank you for your cooperation in this matter.

Sincerely,

Your Name

Enclosure

Chapter 14: Sample Complaint Letters

**COMPLAINT LETTER TO
MERCHANT REQUESTING CREDIT FOR AN
UNSATISFACTORY PURCHASE**
(Send this letter immediately after the unsatisfactory purchase
and forward a copy to the credit card issuer
along with a letter similar to the one on the next page)

Return address
Today's date

Name and address of merchant

Dear reader (use correct name if known):

RE: Dissatisfaction with Purchase

I am writing today to complain about a charge from (name of merchant) that appeared on my recent (name of credit card company) bill. This bill is wrong, and I am asking (name of merchant) to credit my account for (amount of credit desired).

The reason for this request is that (give reason). (Explain your side of the situation more fully. If appropriate, explain why you desire a partial credit rather than a full credit.

Therefore, I expect that (name of merchant) will credit my credit card account in the amount of (put amount here) as soon as possible. Thank you for your cooperation in this matter.

With a copy of this letter, I am also officially requesting my credit card issuer to investigate this matter and credit my account under the provisions of the Fair Credit Reporting Act dealing with goods delivered not in the condition as agreed upon. The FCBA
and the contract between (name of merchant *and* the name of the credit card company) both require that my account be immediately credited for the amount challenged while the credit card issuer investigates the complaint. Since my facts as described above are correct, the law also says that the credit on my account will remain.

Thank you for your cooperation in this matter, and (if true, tell them that you intend on doing business with them again.)

Sincerely,

Your Name

P.S. My (name of credit card issuer) credit card account number is (put your number here).

**COMPLAINT LETTER TO
CREDIT CARD COMPANY ABOUT
AN UNSATISFACTORY PURCHASE**
(Send this letter on the same day your letter on
the previous page is sent to the merchant)

Return address
Today's date

Name and address of credit card issuer

Dear reader (use correct name if known):

RE: Credit Card Charge Account #(put your number here)

I am writing today to challenge a charge from (name of merchant) that appeared on my recent bill. The amount of (give dollar figure here) that appeared on my bill with a date of (give date here) is wrong because the goods were not delivered in the condition agreed upon. As you can see from the enclosed letter, I have already attempted to get (name of merchant) to credit my account for (amount of credit desired).

The reason why the amount on my bill is being challenged is that (give reason here). (Explain your side of the situation fully. If appropriate, explain why you are willing to accept a partial credit rather than a full credit.)

Therefore, I expect that (name of credit card company) will immediately credit my account for the challenged amount (and, if appropriate, remove any interest assessed on that particular charge). Plus, (name of credit card company) will investigate this transaction with (name of merchant) and send me a letter reporting the findings. I fully expect that my credit card account with (name of credit card company) will remain credited in the amount of (put amount here).

Thank you for your cooperation in this matter.

Sincerely,

Your Name

Enclosure (copy of letter to merchant)

Chapter 14: Sample Complaint Letters

**SECOND COMPLAINT LETTER TO CREDIT CARD ISSUER
TO DISPUTE AN ITEM ON A CREDIT CARD BILL
(Send this letter if the credit card company
turns down your initial request for a credit)**

Return address
Today's date

Name and address of credit card issuer

Dear supervisor of lower-level employee (at credit card issuer):

RE: Credit Card Charge Account #(put your number here)

Please see the enclosed letters in reference to a charge of (put amount here) on my (name of credit card company) account that I am challenging because it was an unsatisfactory purchase. As you can see from the enclosed correspondence, I have asked the merchant to correct the error. In addition, I have asked (name of credit card company) to correct the error. Your (name of credit card company person who signed letter saying that upon completion of the initial investigation) wrote to me saying that they will not credit my account. I believe that (name of credit card issuer) has made a mistake in initially deciding not to properly credit my account for (repeat the reason given in their letter). Therefore, I am asking that you take corrective action.

(Give your reason[s], such as simply sending you a photocopy of your correct signature does not invalidate your proper claim of defective/shoddy/deficient product or service.)

Should my account not be credited by the next billing cycle and the amount of the original charge remain on the account, I will then file an official complaint to the Federal Trade Commission under the rights provided consumers by the Fair Credit Billing Act. As you know, the FCBA and the contract between (name of merchant *and* the name of the credit card issuer) both require that my account be credited for any amount challenged while the credit card issuer investigates the complaint. I contend that your investigation was insufficient and that the facts of the situation, described in the enclosed letters, are correct. The law says that the credit on my account will remain when the merchant is wrong. If (name of credit card issuer) fails to follow all the government rules within proper time limits, (name of credit card issuer) is required by law to credit my account for $50 of the amount in dispute. Alternatively, I can sue (name of credit card issuer) in the local small claims court and ask that court to order the credit, plus attorney fees and costs.

Further, (name of credit card issuer) will not lose a penny on this complaint since all you have to do is process your credit against (name of merchant) as detailed in your contractual agreement with that merchant.

If, after reinvestigating this complaint, (name of credit card issuer) still does not credit my account I will close my account. If I close my account, (name of credit card issuer) will lose approximately (amount of dollars here based upon last year's total finance charges) from interest charges plus (amount of dollars here based on three percent of last year's total purchases) from discounts to retailers for each charge. That means (name of credit card issuer) will lose (total amount of both figures) if my account is not properly credited.

Therefore, I expect that (name of credit card issuer) will credit my account for the challenged amount (and, if appropriate, remove any interest assessed on that particular charge).

Thank you very much for your cooperation in this matter.

Sincerely,

Your Name

Enclosures

EXAMPLE OF A "CONSUMER STATEMENT" TO ADD TO ONE'S CREDIT REPORT TO TELL THE CONSUMER'S SIDE OF A DISPUTE
(Up to 200 may be added to one's credit file)

                                      Return address
                                      Today's date

Name and address of credit bureau (TRW, Equifax, or Transunion)

Dear reader (use correct name if known)

Please add the following consumer statement to my credit file:

"Last year, I co-leased an apartment for one year with a friend. One week before our lease expired, I moved back to my hometown. Prior to my departure, I called the leasing agent for the apartment complex and confirmed that I owed nothing on the lease. However, unbeknownst to me, my former roommate had damaged the apartment in the process of moving out. In addition, he remained in the apartment five days beyond the date of the expiration of the lease. He further chose not to pay the realty agent for those expenses. Six months later, the XYZ Collection Agency notified me that I was responsible for the $300 not paid by my former roommate. I promptly paid them."

After this consumer statement is added to my credit file, please send me a copy of my credit report. Thank you for your cooperation in this matter.

                                      Sincerely,

                                      Your Name

Chapter 15

Agencies and Organizations That Help Protect Consumers

There are literally hundreds of organizations and agencies that can assist in resolving consumer problems. This chapter includes a list of some of the major trade associations and federal government agencies that may be helpful.

Consumer's Resource Handbook

The federal government's U.S. Office of Consumer Affairs publishes the *Consumer's Resource Handbook* every year. In addition to offering tips on buying smart, it provides thousands of addresses in a consumer assistance directory format. Included are corporations, national consumer organizations, car manufacturers, Better Business Bureaus, trade associations, government consumer protection offices, aging offices, banking authorities, insurance regulators, securities administrators, utility commissions, vocational and rehabilitation offices, weights and measures offices, selected federal agencies, and military commissary and exchange offices. Single copies are available free by writing: Consumer's Resource Handbook, Consumer Information Center, Pueblo, Colorado 81009. Copies are often available at libraries and on military bases.

Federal Government Agencies That Help Consumers

A number of federal agencies have consumer affairs responsibilities. It is important to realize that federal agencies cannot help resolve specific individual consumer complaints. However, federal agencies need to hear from consumers about the problems they are experiencing so that they can design and implement programs to help all consumers.

After being recorded at the federal level, many complaints are referred to other more appropriate agencies, often state and local, that might offer specific types of assistance. They might suggest you communicate with another federal agency, a state consumer protection agency, a private consumer action organization, or an attorney. Federal agencies should be contacted to alert them to the existence of specific consumer problems, particularly if such problems might affect a large number of people nationwide. The consumer-related aspects of federal agencies are noted below.

Commission on Civil Rights
1121 Vermont Avenue, NW
Washington, D.C. 20425

>The Commission on Civil Rights enforces federal laws on discrimination, for example, in the areas of housing and credit.

Commodity Futures Trading Commission
2033 K Street, NW
Washington, DC 20581

>The Commodity Futures Trading Commission (CFTC) is an independent agency that regulates trading in commodities and certain other investment transactions, such as options. The agency works to prevent market manipulation and to protect customers who buy and sell commodities contracts. Through its procedures, consumers can make claims against brokers and salespeople.

Comptroller of the Currency
Department of the Treasury
490 L'Enfant Plaza, S.W.
Washington, D.C. 20219

> The Comptroller of the Currency is part of the Department of the Treasury. It handles complaints about national banks, those that have the word "National" in their names or the initials "N.A." after their names.

Consumer Information Center
Pueblo, CO 81009

> The Consumer information Center (CIC) helps provide consumers with information on how to be more effective consumers. The CIC works with federal agencies to determine what kinds of information are available that could help consumers. The CIC encourages other government agencies to publish useful information. The CIC republishes and distributes hundreds of useful booklets, many of which are free. These are listed in its quarterly catalog, *Consumer Information*. You frequently see CIC public service announcements on television requesting that you write Pueblo, Colorado 81009 for a free catalog so you can order publications.

Consumer Product Safety Commission
Washington, D.C. 20207

> The Consumer Product Safety Commission (CPSC) is an independent regulatory agency that protects consumers against unreasonable risks from most consumer products used around the home or in schools or recreation areas. The CPSC does this by developing standards for consumer products, promoting research, and assisting consumers in evaluating the comparative safety of products. The CPSC has jurisdiction over more than 10,000 products and enforces specific laws regulating flammable fabrics, packaging of poisonous products, hazardous substances, and refrigerator safety. It does not have jurisdiction over food, drugs, cosmetics, medical devices, motor vehicles, boats, firearms, alcohol, tobacco, pesticides, or aircraft. The CPSC can seek court action to ban particularly hazardous products, as well as write regulations to ban classes of hazardous products and to establish mandatory safety standards. The CPSC handles complaints about product-related deaths, injuries, and illnesses.

Department of Agriculture
Office of the Consumer Advisor
Washington, D.C. 20250

> The U.S. Department of Agriculture (USDA) has the responsibility to ensure that meat and poultry products are safe, wholesome, and truthfully labeled. The USDA inspects meat and poultry, as well as products made from them in packing, housing, and processing plants. The USDA checks for sanitation problems, proper labeling, and correct use of food additives. The USDA provides voluntary grading services for meat, poultry, eggs, dairy products, and some fresh and processed foods and vegetables. The USDA handles complaints about meat and poultry products except for advertising. The USDA also provides information and education about these topics and others to consumers through the Cooperative Extension Service, a national education network operated through land-grant universities with extension professionals in nearly all the nation's 3150 counties located in every state and in U.S. territories.

Department of Commerce
Washington, DC 20233

The Department of Commerce is charged with promoting commerce in the United States. It also enforces a number of laws and regulations. Commerce contains the National Institute of Standards and Technology and the Patent and Trademark Office.

Department of Education
Washington, D.C. 20202

The Department of Education oversees federal student aid programs, and accepts complaints about schools.

Department of Energy
Washington, D.C. 20585

The Department of Energy (DOE) attempts to coordinate national energy policy. It is involved in energy conservation, renewable resources, and technology assistance. Complaints about energy labeling should be directed to the DOE.

Department of Health and Human Services
5600 Fishers Lane
Rockville, MD 20857

The Department of Health and Human Services (HHS) oversees most health policies of the federal government. It contains the Food and Drug Administration, Health Care Financing Administration, and Second Surgical Opinion Program. HHS also has a cancer hotline (800-4-CANCER) to answer queries.

Department of Housing and Urban Development
Washington, D.C. 20410

The Department of Housing and Urban Development (HUD) deals with problems regarding availability and quality of all housing, including manufactured homes. HUD handles complaints about Federal Housing Administration insured home loans, lead-based paint in housing, safety problems with manufactured homes, urban rehabilitation, interstate land sales, fair housing and equal opportunity lending, and federal government subsidized rental housing.

Department of the Interior
Washington, D.C. 20240

The Department of the Interior oversees parks, wildlife, Indian affairs, and land management.

Department of Justice
Washington, D.C. 20530

The Department of Justice is the primary law enforcement agency of the federal government. It has a division to implement federal antitrust laws. Civil rights legislation is also enforced.

Department of Labor
Washington, D.C. 20210

The Department of Labor oversees labor-management relations at the federal level. It deals with employment standards and training, occupational safety and health, and pension and welfare benefits.

Department of State
Washington, D.C. 20520

The Department of State offers emergency and non-emergency overseas citizen services, as well as passport and visa services.

Department of Transportation
Washington, D.C. 20591

The Department of Transportation (DOT) deals with most forms of transportation, including automobiles, airplanes, and trucks. The Consumer Affairs Office of DOT checks on complaints, safety-related problems, and on-time performance.

Department of the Treasury
1200 Pennsylvania Avenue
Washington, D.C. 20226

The Department of Treasury enforces labeling requirements on alcoholic beverages. It also houses the offices of the Comptroller of the Currency, Office of Thrift Supervision, Customs Service, and Internal Revenue Service.

Department of Veterans Affairs
810 Vermont Avenue, N.W.
Washington, D.C. 20420

The Department of Veterans Affairs (VA) oversees programs to benefit veterans, including the cemetery system, health services, and veterans benefits. The VA offers subsidized housing loans.

Environmental Protection Agency
Washington, D.C. 20460

The Environmental Protection Agency (EPA) oversees the nation's environmental policies. It is involved with safe drinking water, pesticides, resource conservation and recovery, and toxic substances.

Equal Employment Opportunity Commission
1801 L Street, N.W.
Washington, D.C. 20507

The Equal Employment Opportunity Commission (EEOC) enforces the nation's civil right laws in the area of employment.

Federal Bureau of Investigation

The Federal Bureua of Investigation may be contacted when a sales offer may involve mail or wire fraud, or other violations of criminal law. Check the "government" listings section of a telephone book to locate the nearest office, or call 1-202-324-3000.

Federal Communications Commission
2025 M Street, N.W.
Washington, D.C. 20554

The Federal Communications Commission (FCC) oversees the nation's telecommunications policies. It accepts complaints about all common carriers of mass communications, including comments on children's advertising. The FCC regulates public access to communication.

Federal Deposit Insurance Corporation
550 17th Street, N.W.
Washington, D.C. 20429

The Federal Deposit Insurance Corporation (FDIC) handles complaints about FDIC-insured banks, savings and loan associations, and credit unions.

Federal Reserve Board
Division of Consumer and Community Affairs
Washington, D.C. 20551

The Federal Reserve Board is the agency that coordinates the nation's banking policies. This independent agency handles consumer complaints about financial institutions that are members of the Federal Reserve System. It oversees a number of federal laws and regulations, such as Truth in Savings, Equal Credit Opportunity Act, and the Truth in Lending Act.

Federal Trade Commission
Washington, D.C. 20580

The Federal Trade Commission (FTC) enforces antitrust and warranty laws and consumer protection statutes, including those prohibiting false advertising and fraud in credit lending. They are responsible for preventing unfair, false, or deceptive advertisements, and for promoting fair competition. Any complaint about advertising, fabric care labeling, energy-efficiency and food product labeling should go to the FTC. It also takes complaints about credit and warranty legislation, as well as violations of mail-order regulations.

Food and Drug Administration
5600 Fishers Lane
Rockville, MD 20857

The Food and Drug Administration (FDA) enforces laws to ensure the purity and safety of foods (other than meat and poultry), drugs, and cosmetics, the safety of therapeutic devices, and the truthful, informative labeling of such products. Food additives, color additives, antibiotic drugs, insulin, and most prescription drugs are subject to premarket approval by the agency. The FDA handles complaints about food, food additives, prescription drugs, over-the-counter drugs, cosmetics, and medical devices, except for advertising.

Interstate Commerce Commission
Washington, D.C. 20423

The Interstate Commerce Commission (ICC) is responsible for regulating the interstate shipment of goods using surface transportation, such as trucks, buses, railroads, oil pipelines, express companies, freight forwarders, and railroads. It also accepts complaints about interstate moving companies.

National Association of Securities Dealers
1735 K Street, NW
Washington, DC 20006-1500

The National Association of Securities Dealers is the self-regulatory group that has disciplinary information about stockbrokers and brokerage firms.

National Association of Insurance Commissioners
120 W. 12th Street, Suite 1100
Kansas City, MO 64105

The National Association of Insurance Commissioners provides single copies of free shopper's guides on various types of insurance policies, such as health, cancer, auto and long-term care.

National Credit Union Administration
1776 G Street, NW
Washington, D.C. 20456

The National Credit Union Administration (NCUA) handles consumer complaints about federally insured credit unions.

National Fraud Information Center
815 15th Street, NW
Washington, D.C. 20005

The National Credit Information Center can be contacted for information, referrals and assistance in filing complaints.

National Futures Association
200 West Madison Street, Suite 1600
Chicago, IL 60606-3570

The National Futures Association is the self-regulatory organization for investments of futures contracts, and they maintain a data bank of disciplinary action on individuals and firms that sell futures contract.

National Institute of Standards and Technology
Department of Commerce
Washington, D.C. 20234

The Department of Commerce is responsible for the promotion of American goods and services both at home and abroad. An important agency within the department is the National Institute of Standards and Technology (NIST), which assists industry in the development of technology and procedures needed to improve quality. It has a central laboratory for developing and disseminating measurement standards and scientific data.

National Highway Traffic Safety Administration
Department of Transportation
Washington, D. C. 20609

The National Highway Traffic Safety Administration (NHTSA) is responsible for developing minimum performance standards and enforcing safety regulations that promote motor vehicle safety. Its jurisdiction includes automobiles, trucks, buses, recreational vehicles, motorcycles, bicycles, mopeds, and all related accessory equipment. NHTSA's efforts are aimed at reducing highway deaths, injuries, and associated property losses particularly through pursuit of allegations about vehicle defects. It is an administrative unit in the Department of Transportation, and it publishes (but does not have jurisdiction over) the gas mileage performance averages of individual vehicles. NHTSA is well known for its automobile recall program because it encourages voluntary recalls and occasionally orders mandatory recalls by manufacturers when safety problems are discovered. It handles complaints about automobile safety, automobile recalls, concerns about automobile design, and fuel economy ratings.

Occupational Safety and Health Administration
Department of Labor
200 Constitution Avenue, N.W.
Washington, D.C. 20210

The Occupational Safety and Health Administration (OSHA) has responsibility for safety and health in the workplace. OSHA issues standards for work hazards.

Office of Thrift Supervision
Department of the Treasury
1700 G Street, N.W.
Washington, D.C. 20552

The Office of Thrift Supervision is located in the Department of the Treasury. It handles complaints about savings and loan associations and savings banks.

Pension Benefit Guaranty Corporation
2020 K Street, N.W.
Washington, D.C. 20006

The Pension Benefit Guaranty Corporation is the federal agency that insures a great number

Securities and Exchange Commission
Washington, D.C. 20549

The Securities and Exchange Commission (SEC) is an independent regulatory agency that oversees investment companies, investment advisors, stockbrokers and dealers, and the operation of stock markets. The SEC is responsible for setting up and enforcing regulations that prevent fraud in the securities markets. The SEC handles complaints about dishonesty, malpractice, and unfair actions in the securities industry.

U.S. Office of Consumer Affairs
750 17th Street, NW, 6th Floor
Washington, D.C. 20006

The U.S. Office of Consumer Affairs (USOCA) tries to coordinate all federal activities on behalf of consumers. It plans, organizes, and publicizes National Consumers Week. USOCA publishes the *Consumer's Resource Handbook*, a where-to-go, how-to-do-it question and complaint manual for consumers that is available free by writing the Consumer Information Center. USOCA's director is also special adviser to the President for Consumer Affairs; chairperson of the Consumer Affairs Council, an organization of federal agency consumer representatives; and head of the U.S. delegation to semiannual meetings of the Committee on Consumer Policy of the Organization of Economic Cooperation and Development in Paris.

U.S. Postal Service
Washington, D.C. 20260

The U.S. Postal Service is an independent agency responsible for investigating mail fraud and other mail-related user problems. The Postal Service enforces laws and regulations aimed at stopping mail fraud, prohibiting unordered merchandise, and obscenity. Complaints involving mail are handled by all postmasters, but they may be forwarded to the U.S. Postal Service Consumer Advocate in Washington.

State, County and City Government Offices That Help Consumers

All states have a number of government offices that help consumers. If there is no local consumer office in your area, contact the state consumer protection office which is located in the capital city of the state. State consumer protection offices are located in one or more places: (1) the "Department of Consumer Affairs," (2) the "Attorney General's Office," or (3) the "Governor's Office." Most have toll-free telephone numbers. The telephone numbers for all such offices may be easily obtained from directory assistance (AREA CODE + 555-1212).

Other state offices that help with specific consumer problems are also located in state capital cities. These include state (1) "Agencies on Aging" that coordinate services for older Americans, (2) "Banking Authorities" that regulate state-chartered banks and other financial institutions, (3) "Insurance Regulators" that oversee all types of insurance companies, (4) "Securities Administrators" to regulate stocks, bonds and real estate transactions, (5) "Utility Commissions" that regulate customer service and prices, (6) "Weights and Measures Offices" that regulate labels, weights, measures and counts (i.e., supermarket scales, gasoline pumps, taxicab meters, rental car odometers), (7) "Occupational and Professional Licensing Boards" that register and discipline members of various professions and occupations, and (8) "Regional Military Commissary and Exchange Offices."

Trade Association Resolution Programs

Most businesses are willing to respond to consumer complaints in an attempt to resolve disagreements. The Better Business Bureau, a non-profit organization sponsored by local businesses, has over 200 offices nationally. Key services that they offer include answering consumer inquiries about companies' consumer complaint records and mediating disputes between sellers and consumers. Some offer arbitration.

Companies that manufacturer similar products often establish trade association resolution programs to resolve differences between their member companies and consumers. Some major groups are listed below.

Automotive Consumer Action Program (AUTOCAP)
8400 Westpark Drive
McLean, VA 22102

Better Business Bureau Autoline
Council of Better Business Bureaus
1515 Wilson Boulevard
Arlington, VA 22209

Better Business Bureau National Consumer Arbitration
Council of Better Business Bureaus
1515 Wilson Boulevard
Arlington, VA 22209

Carpet and Rug Institute
1100 17th Street, NW
Washington, DC 20036

Cemetery Consumer Service Council
P.O. Box 3574
Washington, DC 20007

Direct Marketing Association
Mail Order Action Line
1101 17th Street, NW - Suite 705
Washington, DC 20036

Direct Selling Association
1776 K Street, NW
Washington, DC 20006

Electronic Industries Association
Consumer Electronics Group
2001 Eye Street, NW
Washington, DC 20006

Funeral Service Consumer Action Program (FSCAP)
11121 West Oklahoma Avenue
Milwaukee, WI 53227

Furniture Industry Consumer Action Panel (FICAP)
HP-7
High Point, NC 27261

Home Owners Warranty Program (HOW)
2000 L Street, NW
Washington, DC 20036

Household Goods Dispute Settlement Program
400 Army-Navy Drive
Arlington, VA 22202

International Association for Financial Planning
2 Concourse Parkway, Suite 800
Atlanta, GA 30328

Major Appliance Consumer Action Panel (MACAP)
20 North Wacker Drive
Chicago, IL 60606

National Advertising Division (NAD)
Council of Better Business Bureaus
845 Third Avenue
New York, NY 10022